Navigating Conflict

Navigating Conflict

Tools for Difficult Conversations

Lynne Curry, PhD

BEP

BUSINESS EXPERT PRESS

Leader in applied, concise business books

Navigating Conflict: Tools for Difficult Conversations

Copyright © Lynne Curry, 2022

Cover design by Charlene Kronstedt

Interior design by Exeter Premedia Services Private Ltd., Chennai, India

First published in 2022 by
Business Expert Press, LLC
222 East 46th Street, New York, NY 10017
www.businessexpertpress.com

ISBN-13: 978-1-63742-338-7 (paperback)
ISBN-13: 978-1-63742-339-4 (e-book)

Business Expert Press Human Resource Management and Organizational Behavior Collection

First edition: 2022

10 9 8 7 6 5 4 3 2 1

To Ben Swann, the best son I could hope for.

To God, who provides strength, comfort, and wisdom.

To the delightful Jenny, Parker, MaHayla, and Cooper.

Description

Navigating Conflict: Tools for Difficult Conversations gives readers a life-changing, self-training manual for navigating difficult conflicts and situations. This book is perfect for readers that want positive outcomes from personal, professional, and workplace conflicts.

Written by a nationally respected trainer and coach, *Navigating Conflict* provides readers a toolbox chock-full of practical, effective, innovative, easy-to-apply skills and strategies.

In this workbook-like guide, you will gain:

- A step-by-step roadmap for handling conflict and defusing tough and touchy situations.
- Strategies for achieving productive outcomes to conflict.
- Strategies for effectively handling yourself under fire.
- Skills for making conflict work for you.
- Tools for dealing with toxic individuals, personality conflicts, office politics, and problematic personal situations.
- Tools for handling criticism and attacking comments.
- Tools for raising problem issues so they can be resolved.

Written in a straight-forward, relatable, engaging manner, *Navigating Conflict* is designed to enable readers to return to specific chapters for a quick reference when they need an immediate tactic or strategy. Readers will find the real-life stories engrossing, the skills immediately actionable, and will walk away knowing exactly how to achieve positive outcomes in conflict situations.

Keywords

managing and handling conflict; conflict resolution; conflict management; office politics; personality conflicts; interpersonal relationships; personal development; workplace bullies; crucial conversations

Other Books by Lynne Curry

Managing for Accountability: A Business Leader's Toolbox, Business Expert Press, 2021

Beating the Workplace Bully: A Tactical Guide to Taking Charge, AMACOM, 2016

Solutions, Communication Works Inc., 2006 and 2012

Won By One, Communication Works, Inc., 2002

Managing Equally and Legally, McFarland & Company, 1990

Contents

Testimonials

"How I wish I had the opportunity to read Dr. Lynne Curry's most recent book, Navigating Conflict: Tools for Difficult Conversations *a few months ago! Over the past months, I've voyaged through numerous large and small conflicts. There is no doubt that Curry's sage advice and guidance helped me maintain a steady course during those challenging times. I'm certain some of the conflicts I encountered would not have been resolved without her help and valuable insights.*

Curry's newest book is a field guide to identify those uncomfortable situations where one may fall short in personal confidence or past experiences to deal with conflict. She pulls back the curtain of self-doubt to show you relatable strategies to positively overcome and resolve those uncomfortable encounters. As an added bonus, you find your confidence and strategic thinking strengthening. Curry has done a splendid job of drawing upon her decades of experience to help you address and resolve conflict. I have learned many lessons from Curry, and this is another of her superb writings that will become a go-to textbook."—**Dr. James Powell, President, Clearwater Marine Aquarium**

"No one understands how to handle and manage conflict like Lynne Curry, and no one writes about it better. If you ever have to deal with conflict (and you will), Curry's book helps you identify and improve how you handle conflict. This is a must read."—**Sean Eichrodt, Securities and Investigations Management, The GEO Group**

"When I read the 1st page of this book, I knew it would be my 'Bible' when 'Navigating Conflict.' In our organization. I immediately was able to equate 'On the Ground Situations' I had experienced over the past 30+ years of managing people with the examples Curry presented. I quickly grabbed my highlighter and started madly highlighting key areas of interest. This is not just a book to read but a book to have at arm's length as a reference when you know you're about to enter in a situation that may be confrontational. Use

the book as a guide and it will make your organization more productive and give you a 'peace of mind' when you leave work each day."—**Joel Klessens, President, Alaska Mill and Feed**

"*Lynne Curry's new book,* Navigating Conflict: Tools for Difficult Conversations, *is a gem. Filled with effective and practical advice for touchy and tricky situations, this book is a must for anyone wanting to tool up and become more effective communicators both personally and professionally. Curry's writing is both engaging and empowering.*

Curry has a knack for connecting with the reader and taking us on a journey through her powerful storytelling that weaves in simple solutions for difficult situations. I will be adding this book to my permanent library along with her equally seminal book, Beating the Workplace Bully.*"*
—**Jessie Sutherland, author of *Worldview Skills: Transforming Conflict from the Inside Out* and Director of Intercultural Strategies and TEDx Speaker**

"Navigating Conflict: Tools for Difficult Conversations *is a must-read for anyone in a leadership role. The story-based format is founded on real-life examples and draws from Lynne Curry's four decades of experience. I found myself shaking my head in agreement and relating to similar situations I had experienced and wished I had had the information in this book to help navigate those past conflicts.*

Dr. Curry actively engages the reader each step of the way by asking probing questions and providing exercises that the reader can immediately use at home or in the workplace. In addition, Dr. Curry conveys to the reader complex concepts with ease, such as building the necessary skills needed when being faced with criticism challenges. From just the first few pages, I had already started building my toolkit."—**Lisa Oliver, Chief Operating Officer, Clearwater Marine Aquarium**

"*Dr. Lynne Curry has been an invaluable resource throughout my career. She combines empathy and a no-nonsense solution-oriented approach to business and interpersonal development. Her writings incorporate the experiences from her distinguished career giving the reader insight into specific and very real situations.*

Unlike many management self-help writers, Curry delivers each lesson in three distinct touch points including a brief interactive section. I can't emphasize how critical that is for retention and implementation in the real world. Navigating Conflict: Tools for Difficult Conversations *is a must read for anyone looking for advice on tackling the tough situations and conversations the hit us in both the management world and our personal lives.*"—**Jed Shandy, Vice President, Davis Constructors and Engineers**

"*Dr. Lynne Curry has done it again! For the past 25 years, my teams and I have been the recipient of Curry's practical approach to unlocking the potential of our workforce and understanding our team's interpersonal dynamics. I have personally learned and developed so many life skills from Curry's instruction, coaching, and mentoring. Her new book,* Navigating Conflict, *is not just a 'must-read' but a resource that you will want to keep handy for frequent reference.*

You will find a concentration of pragmatic, yet idealistic, tools and approaches to recognizing, understanding, and responding to conflict in the workplace and beyond. This book will help you develop self-awareness in a way that has you stand up for yourself candidly and professionally while understanding what it is like being on the other side of you.

It will concomitantly increase your awareness of others in an empathic way that prefers to call others 'up' and not 'out.' This best-of-breed concentration of conflict tools accompanied by Curry's real-life application, experience, and lessons learned will become my new go-to for both personal and team development and improvement. You'll want to get your copy and start augmenting your conflict management skills as well as those of the teams you lead and/or participate in."—**Jim Bates, President and CEO of BIG-Business Improvement Group, Inc.**

"Navigating Conflict: Tools for Difficult Conversations *is a book I wish I would have had at the beginning of my management career. Dr. Curry uses her vast experience and real-life examples to succinctly describe how tough issues can be managed appropriately.*

Curry's practical and understandable strategies show the reader how to manage issues head-on while still considering other's points of view and our own biases. This book has already helped me recognize how I can better confront conflict in a timely manner that does not sacrifice my own opinions or values.

Her helpful exercises at the end of the chapters and real-life examples from her years of experience in HR consultation are engaging and helpful, like having Dr. Curry working side-by-side with us in these difficult situations. All of this information is packaged in an interesting and engaging manner. Thank you for this wonderful resource!"—**Debbie Davey, Director of Risk Management, Cross Road Health Ministries, Inc.**

"Lynne Curry has done it again! Lynne's latest book, Navigating Conflict: Tools for Difficult Conversations, *is an excellent read. It is another great primer by Curry for all who read it on how to deal constructively with conflicts in all walks of life. Although Curry focuses her examples upon the work environment, her counseling on conflict resolution has universal application— be it the workplace, social interactions, or even the family. Recognizing that time is valuable, Curry has encapsulated her coaching into concise, easy-to-understand common sense chapters. I highly recommend Curry's book to anyone who wants to improve their approach to dispute resolution at whatever level and situation."*—**William Satterberg, J.D., owner, Law Offices of William Satterberg, Jr.**

"Lynne Curry gives you clear, concise, and current advice on how to chart a course through the rough seas of interpersonal conflict. Using real-life examples, Navigating Conflict *helps you understand motivations of other people (and yourself). The book is packed with self-tests, exercises, and checklists to help you overcome old behaviors and bring your best attitudes to interactions with others. This book will help you develop strategies for navigating through conflict in the workplace and off-the-job."*—**Barbara Manning Grimm, Managing Editor for Plain Language Media, the publishers of Medical Office Manager and Law Office Manager**

"If you are working with others, have interpersonal relationships of any kind, or are in the workforce, you want to read this book. With our world so full of conflict, from personal to political issues, Dr. Lynne Curry's newest book will help you navigate the challenges. Navigating Conflict *gives you a*

roadmap to success in dealing with conflict and demanding situations with employees, co-workers, and in the workplace and at home.

I write this as a business leader with 35 plus years working in the resource and technology industry, government, and the nonprofit sector. I have been an avid reader of Curry's books and have found multiple answers to concerns I experienced during my career, thanks to her insightfulness and 40 years of experience counseling clients and business leaders worldwide. I recommend buying this book for yourself and your friends who confide in you about workplace issues. You are surely to find this book full of inspiration, and insightful, creative, and thoughtful answers."—**Rebecca Parker, Executive Director, Anchorage Senior Activity Center, Alaska**

"Dr. Curry's Navigating Conflict *provides real-world tools for managers facing the daily challenges of our complex and ever evolving workplaces. The skills attained from the lessons presented here are extremely valuable to our personal as well as our work lives. Curry provides practical tools and effective strategies for managing myself as well as employees. Her book thus benefits me and everyone I encounter, home or office. I'm grateful for this book; it's a gift I keep on my desk."*—**Randall Kowalke, Chief Executive Officer, Sunshine Community Health Services**

"We all experience conflict. Through a wealth of real-life examples and action suggestions, Curry helps me understand conflict and how we can better manage and use conflict to enjoy more profitable, and happier relationships. This book is full of relatable lessons Curry shares from her 40 years of consulting and training in organizations. The knowledge Curry shares has inspired me to look at conflict in new ways, and through this, helps me to understand and manage it in ways that benefit not only me, but those around me."
—**Barbara Elfman Bell, Chief People and Culture Officer, Rural Alaska Community Action Program**

"Dr. Curry does it again! Curry has a unique way of asking questions that makes you reflect inward and have light bulbs turn on! Her book, Navigating Conflict, *provides a practical guide to use at work or at home; to use with coworkers, personal acquaintances, or to provide self-recognition. Curry gives*

you a little bit of herself in the 'YOUR TURN—ACTION STEPS' at the end of each chapter. You can hear her coaching you through different scenarios. Through Navigating Conflict, *Curry provides you the tools to turn challenges into learning moments, and then into growth opportunities. This is a must-read, must practice, and must share book!"*—**Kimberly McCourtney, Sr Vice President, Alaska Mill Feed & Garden Center**

"Curry writes with a direct approach that is refreshing. In a professional world fraught with political correctness, creating paralysis among managers concerned about taking a misstep, Curry takes an approach that gives life to how conflict can and should be handled—both personally and professionally. Reading this shows individuals how to take control of situations that they otherwise may avoid—and 'gives permission' to professionals to direct criticism and conflict down a productive path where resolution can occur."
—**Wendy Yow, Vice President of Human Resources, Credit Union 1**

"Curry's Navigating Conflict *is written in a conversational format that makes for easy reading. That is not to say it is easy in that it challenges the reader to dig deep and recognize the part they play in conflict. Within minutes I was seeing myself in several of the situations and realizing there were things that I could have done differently to get a much better outcome. This will be a book that I will be recommending to my team and others!"*—**Michele Sommer, Global Employee Relations Leader in a leading technology company**

"In four decades as a management consultant, workplace coach, and expert witness, Lynne Curry has shown her expertise in dealing with difficult situations. In Navigating Conflict: Tools for Difficult Conversations, *she provides practical guidance in managing conflict. This book provides strategies and tools for handling conflicts in the workplace and personal life, with real world examples and concrete action steps. Topics include responding to criticism, understanding your stories, and dealing with difficult individuals. No matter what your position is, you will benefit from this book."*—**Harry Cylinder, CPCU, ARM, Risk and Insurance Consultant, Beacon Insurance Services LLC**

"In this immediately useful book, Lynne Curry teaches valuable tools for standing up for yourself and strengthening your backbone muscles. Put these exercises into practice; rehearse with a friend or a workmate, and you'll see clear benefits. You'll make the relationships with good character colleagues even stronger by having real discussions. And these same techniques will help you disarm bad-faith actors and bullies. I heartily recommend this book."
—**Ramji Srinivasan, Founder and CEO at Teiko.bio**

"This is the book we all need to read! In Navigating Conflict, *Dr. Lynne Curry provides a practical, how-to manual for dealing with professional and personal conflict. Reading the book requires critical self-analysis that can lead to more productive relationships at work and at home. If you read this book, you will understand the role you have played in the conflicts in your life and a pathway to resolve those conflicts."*—**Clint Campion, J.D., Partner, Sedor Wendlandt Evans Filippi**

"Conflict always seems like something aggressive and unkind, but if you read Lynne Curry's Navigating Conflict, *her practical tools will help you become the most trusted and followed leader and colleague. Most people want to know where they stand with you and this book will help you communicate clearly and early on to defuse relationship issues and create an environment of clear communication. You will find if you apply these practical tools in all areas of your life. Your relationships will be stronger, and you will feel like you have a voice and be able to use it."*—**Trisha Blake, M.S., Chief Marketing Officer**

*"*Navigating Conflict *by Lynne Curry is about how to make your business more successful by making employee–employer relationships more productive. Curry does this with relevant, true-to-life examples of conflicts on the job and then provides a host of tools to help managers and employees see both sides of every situation. Then she gives managers suggestions on how to communicate their own views in ways that lead to understanding and agreement instead of unproductive impasses or dictatorial declarations. Interestingly enough, the same solutions that help managers and their employees be more accountable on the job, work equally well when dealing with conflicts at home. Because*

ultimately, this book helps readers deal better with people, whatever their position, relationship or situation."—**Wendy Lalli, Principal, Words & Beyond, LLC**

"A large percentage of problems in the workplace stem from the avoidance of, or the inability to effectively handle, conflict. Confronting and pro-actively dealing with conflict is a skill set that few inherently possess. In Navigating Conflict: Tools for Difficult Conversations. *Lynne Curry provides us with a common-sense, practical, and very useable tool set for improving our conflict-handling skills. While the lessons of this book are most beneficial to handling workplace conflict, the skills acquired will benefit the reader in all aspects of their life where conflict may arise. I will heartily recommend it to all my clients."*—**William Evans, J.D., Partner, Sedor Wendlandt Evans Filippi**

"Lynne Curry's decades of expertise in human relations and conflict resolution are on full display in Navigating Conflict. *She provides insight into why conflict occurs and provides actual tactics and techniques for resolving conflict and tension in relationships, whether at or outside of work. This is a logical, as well as emotional, portrayal of the genesis of conflict, how they peak and how they fester or blowup and how to successfully resolve them. Spoiler alert: Curry's book is not intended as a passive reading activity. Curry requires the reader to critically analyze their own experiences, and what to work on or get beyond, and how to do that. If the reader puts the work in, Curry's strategies and insights will improve their conflict resolution skills as well as their life."*
—**Charles Krugel, J.D., Charles A. Krugel Labor and Employment Law on Behalf of Business**

*"*Navigating Conflict *provides very helpful advice about the art of listening, which is very helpful in the contexts of the workplace, marriages, and for an attorney like myself, to learn information from witnesses, and/or negotiating and resolving problems with opposing parties. I appreciated learning the tools of paraphrasing and matching to enhance rapport, communication, and trust, as well as the types of questions to employ for resolving conflicts.* Navigating Conflict *also provides helpful advice about stating facts versus judgments and setting up guardrails (cooling down) and maintaining the big picture before giving feedback."*—**Kenneth Gutsch, Attorney, Law Offices of Richmond & Quinn**

"Navigating Conflict *is both valuable and extremely compelling. I loved the "discovering the stories you tell yourself," Curry's succinct writing and how she peppers the book with real-life examples that bring her points home."*—**Maxwell Mercer, M.S., Deputy Director, Community Connections, Inc.**

"Navigating Conflict *gives readers both the courage and the tools to communicate effectively during conflict."*—**Tiffany Van Horn, BU President at Corix Group of Companies**

Foreword

You're reading this book by my friend Lynne Curry for one of a few reasons—you either want to help yourself for the future just in case you have to deal with THAT co-worker, you're dealing with that difficult person now, or maybe you're trying to figure out why you've had trouble with certain people in the past.

When I began to write my first book, *The Arsonist in the Office: Fireproofing Your Life Against Toxic Coworkers, Bosses, Employees, and Culture*, I researched and quickly learned that there were many books written on problems in the workplace. Some provided practical tools, others relied on stories, and some were designed for just a manager or an HR professional.

Then there were Lynne Curry's books. When I read Lynne's book, *Beating the Workplace Bully*, she showed the ability to speak to numerous audiences, provide relevant information, and showed a knack for providing perspective that can only come with having consulted for some of the most powerful companies in the world in solving very complicated problems.

That's pure gold for readers. No matter who you are, I can tell you that Lynne has dealt with and understands your side of the problem. And keep on reading because she not only understands the problem, but she's about to give you questions to ask to help you solve or prevent them.

This book is going to force you to deal with the bad actions and attitudes of others, but what I like best about it is that Lynne also wants you to deal with what you can control—how you treat others and your inactions or actions that can start up all sorts of additional problems or make existing ones even worse.

That old saying of "It takes two to tango"? It applies every day to long-term messes in the workplace.

- The young employee who got burned by their manager years ago becomes a manager years later but doesn't recognize they've exactly adopted the management style they resented.

We can either understand what makes them tick—or react when the timebomb of their temper stops ticking and blows.

- Or the employee who is bitter, angry, and disconnected. We treat them as landmines to avoid, or we can become friends, allies, or at least come to an ability to work together if we simply understood their past life experiences that brought them to that point.

Or we can do nothing and simply blame it all on them. We live in a world full of choices, but this book will help you make good ones about the things you deal with daily.

Communication matters. Understanding matters. And learning from the mistakes we make, the patterns of errors we make that we can either analyze or ignore, and creating better habits matters. Listening well and practicing the Golden Rule of good workplace communications habits matters too.

Trust me when I say that Lynne Curry's experience as a workplace consultant on an international stage, her hard work helping millions of people through her columns and blogs, and her ability to equip you for the toughest situations and conversations will help you deal with tough times.

As someone who wrote a book about my experience inside a toxic workplace, I can tell you I did it so others would understand more about how to think and what to understand when they're in the toughest, high-stress moments.

Lynne's provided the same types of tools, techniques, and stories in the pages to follow. Soak it up, use it, and let her smart perspectives protect and position you for great things to come.

—Pete Havel
President, Fireproofed Leadership
Author, *The Arsonist in the Office: Fireproofing Your Life Against Toxic Coworkers, Bosses, Employees, and Cultures*

Acknowledgments

To my grandfather and dad, Ruben and George, strong, kind, and loving men who stood for integrity and courage.

To four exceptional peer reviewers:

Wendy Lalli, a warm, supportive, and wise woman and marketing guru;

Barb Manning Grimm, a solid, skilled editor who publishes excellent magazines and offers her authors on-target assistance;

Anne Cain, an exceptional editor who catches everything;

Richard Birdsall, who always comes through with integrity and humor and can fix difficult client situations with deft skill.

To the 4,400 clients who have provided thousands of learning opportunities by giving me challenges to fix for 44 years.

To subscribers to www.workplacecoachblog.com who field-tested many of the concepts presented in the book now in your hands.

To Zeke, Deuce, Gracie, and Gabriel who thrust leashes into my hands to encourage "open air thinking" to enhance each day's writing.

PART 1

The Payoff

In these first four chapters you'll learn:

- What this book promises you
- The real price you pay for avoiding conflict
- What stops you from handling conflict
- How to partner with courage

CHAPTER 1

The Promise

Tools for Difficult Conversations

Savannah's Situation

Savannah felt she'd taken care of the problem that had ruined her department's harmony for months when she fired Aaron. Aaron had been an infection, pulling other employees behind closed doors and badmouthing Savannah.

Although Savannah knew none of her other employees liked Aaron, she hadn't understood how much they disrespected her because she'd put up with his problem behavior for nine months. When Aaron started a competing firm and sued Savannah for wrongful termination, she expected her employees to back her.

They didn't.

Savannah's best employees feared they'd be dragged into an ugly legal battle. They looked for new jobs and left.

The weaker employees discovered the lawsuit distracted Savannah, enabling them to get away with problem behavior. After all, they'd watched Aaron get by with much worse.

Savannah needed to learn it wasn't enough to be good at what she did; she needed to learn to stand up for herself.

Too-Nice Norm

Norm faced a different conflict challenge. You know the cartoon in which Wile E. Coyote races to the cliff's edge, giving it his all, his legs wheeling as fast as he can; and then, looks down and realizes there's nothing beneath his feet?

That was Norm's life. No matter how hard he worked, his feet never seemed to land on solid ground. Kent and Matt, his peers on the company's sales team and graduates from the same Ivy League school, collaborated with each other and used dirty tricks to steal clients away from Norm.

Unlike Wile E. Coyote, Norm clung to a golden-rule naiveté. He never fought fire with fire or exposed his peers' actions to his boss. Eventually, his boss fired Norm, saying, "you're a nice guy, but not cut out for sales."

Max and His Mouth

Then, there was Max. He opened his mouth and let words fly, detonating important relationships and decimating career opportunities. Max often regretted what he'd said or done, but by the time he apologized, it was often too late.

What's *your* conflict challenge? Are you someone who:

- ☑ Says the wrong thing at the wrong time?
- ☑ Avoids conflict?
- ☑ Wants to win no matter what it costs?
- ☑ Fears you'll make others mad if you voice what you're really thinking?
- ☑ Tries to compromise even when you shouldn't?
- ☑ Or _____?

In what situations do you need additional conflict tools? Do you need to learn how to:

- ☑ Raise problem issues with a boss who micromanages you?
- ☑ Talk to a friend or family member who always criticizes you?
- ☑ Come right out and say what you mean without it sounding like an accusation?
- ☑ Diplomatically present a problem situation?
- ☑ Or _____?

If you picked up *Navigating Conflict*, you want a better result the next time you face conflict. That's what this book promises: proven strategies and tools you can immediately apply, along with real-world examples that show you how these tools and strategies have worked for others and can prove useful for you.

In these chapters, you'll gain:

- A step-by-step roadmap for handling conflict and tough and touchy situations, regardless of your starting point
- Strategies to effectively handle yourself under fire
- Tools that improve the quality of your relationships at work and home
- Strategies for achieving productive outcomes to conflict
- Methods for turning the tables on manipulators and those who feel they have the upper hand
- How to decode personality conflicts
- Concrete methods for engaging your fighting spirit
- Ways to increase your self-confidence and to calm yourself in any confrontation
- An understanding of your conflict style and the chance to develop new behaviors and skills that work for you
- How to make it through unscathed when dealing with toxic individuals
- A strategy and arsenal for handling attacking comments
- How to handle anger and fear
- The courage you need to face trouble situations
- How to bring up problems so they can be resolved and make it through to successful outcomes

Within minutes after finishing each chapter, you'll be able to put what you've learned to use. Each chapter concludes with "Your Turn," in which the questions you answer provide you with new insights about your own situation and provide you with an opportunity to try out your new skills.

How I Can Make These Promises to You

For 39 years, I ran a nationally respected management consulting company. I worked directly with more than 4,300 organizations in Alaska, Arizona, California, Colorado, Connecticut, Florida, Hawaii,

Illinois, Michigan, New York, Oregon, Texas, Washington, Washington D.C., China, England, Guam, Japan, and Korea. My clients included British Petroleum, Conoco Phillips, the U.S. Department of Defense, and the World Bank. Every strategy and tool you'll find in *Navigating Conflict* has been field-tested and proven successful.

I've qualified to testify in court as an expert witness in the areas of Management Best Practices, Human Resources, and Workplace Issues.

I've coached thousands of individuals on how to handle conflict and helped hundreds of organizations navigate through crisis situations. For three years, I authored "The Workplace Coach" column for sheknows .com and served as coach of the quarter for womenworking.com. I answer real-life reader questions weekly in a "Dear Abby of the Workplace" newspaper column and on www.workplacecoachblog.com.

As result, you'll be able to learn from real-life examples from my four decades of helping others successfully navigate conflict. That said, no anecdote represents any one individual. In all instances, each is a composite of two or three of the many people I've coached, merged into one story. I've changed the names and specific facts out of respect for those I've coached.

I commit to you an enjoyable read and a book from which you can learn and profit.

Your Turn: Action Steps

Let's get started. When you know where you're going and why, you're more likely to get there. By answering these four questions, you'll bring to the surface where you're going and why it matters.

1. What led you to buy this book?
2. What do you hope to gain/learn from it?
3. Does unresolved conflict affect your relationships?
4. What do you hope is different by the time you've finished reading *Navigating Conflict*?

CHAPTER 2

The Price You Pay for Avoiding Conflict

When someone treats you poorly, do you let it go? Do you fear that if you bring the situation up, you might make things worse? Do you push your irritation or hurt aside but chalk it up to the other person having a bad day?

Or do you feel comfortable bringing up situations that annoy or trouble you? Do you quickly address problems when they first surface?

If addressing a conflict feels as risky as jumping out of an airplane without a parachute, consider what your hesitation and fear cost you. When you choose the apparent low-risk certainty of silence over the potential risks of speaking out, think about where that path leads you.

It Doesn't Give You What You Need...

When you avoid conflict, it provides at most temporary relief. It fixes nothing. The situation that troubled you remains. Perhaps you wanted a raise and felt it justified. But because you didn't ask for it, you didn't get it.

Maybe you're irritated because your friend chronically arrives late when you plan something with her. She always arrives with a big smile on her face and hugs you as if it were "no big deal." You hug back, even though her lateness means you miss the beginnings of movies or can't find a seat when you arrive at the restaurant.

Or you're tired of listening to your co-worker complain about your supervisor when you know your co-worker shares blame for the rift between the two of them. But you keep your mouth shut and wind up listening to each of them gripe about the other.

You Become the Problem...

When you bite your tongue and choke your feelings down, they often bubble up to the surface. Instead of talking things out, you send out an unhappy vibe. When you keep your grievances to yourself because you don't want to damage your relationships, it backfires. The longer your frustration seeps out, the more it damages the situation and your relationship.

The Problem Festers...

Unresolved conflict sends out tentacles that wrap around your brain and choke the life out of relationships. Unaddressed conflict festers. It's as if you discovered a package of rancid chicken and put it back in the fridge, hoping the chill temperatures would improve it. Soon, the smell infects everything else in the fridge.

The Smoldering Conflict Flares...

Unresolved conflict acts like tinder, ready to ignite into a messy explosion at the worst possible times.

You put off asking for a raise; and then learn your boss hired a new employee at your same salary, even though you'd worked three years for the company. When you're asked to train the new employee, you explode.

Because you waited for your late-arriving friend, you both wind up standing outside the theater doors until the first intermission. When you hear others raving about the first act as they move through the doors, you blow up at your friend and she stalks off—no doubt expecting an apology tomorrow.

Your co-worker finally tells your supervisor about his grievances in front of you and expects you to back him up. When you don't, he feels you betrayed him. You try to explain you didn't see things the same way he did. You learn he took your former silence as agreement, and now won't talk to you.

You Don't Develop Your Conflict Muscles...

You become so practiced at letting things go that you don't develop your conflict resolution muscles. They become flabby, like biceps that should be able to lift 12-pound weights but can't even handle 2-pounders. When you need your conflict resolution muscles, you won't be able to pull them into action.

You Let Yourself Down...

The realization that you don't tackle problems or stick up for yourself hangs over you like a dark cloud. You disappoint yourself and worse, lose respect for yourself.

You also pay an opportunity cost. Disagreement brings with it the opportunity to examine situations and opens up new possibilities and thoughts. When you and another person disagree on strategies and perspectives, it can lead to creative solutions and better decisions.

You Leave Yourself Out...

When you avoid conflict, you forget you have rights. Remember:

- You have the right to respect
- You have the right to speak up and be listened to and to be taken seriously
- You have the right to your feelings and opinions

Sticker Shock...

If you have something to say or an action you need to take, but don't, you may pay a hefty price. The skills, strategies, and tools you pick up in *Navigating Conflict* will help you avoid these costs.

Your Turn: Action Steps

1. What price do you pay for avoiding conflict? Circle each of the following that apply:
   a. Do you disappoint yourself?
   b. Does the problem remain, leaving you to face the worsened unresolved problem in the future?

(Continues)

(Continued)

> c. Do others see you as the problem?
>
> d. Do you risk an emotional flare up?
>
> e. _____
>
> 2. Conflict avoiders believe "biting one's tongue" is safer and wiser than speaking up. When is it not and why?
>
> 3. Let's get a sense of you in terms how you avoid or resolve conflict. Please circle true or false to the following statements:
>
>   a. I put off returning phone calls or e-mails if I don't want to deal with someone. T or F
>
>   b. I bite my tongue when I know I should give my opinion. T or F
>
>   c. To avoid getting into problem discussions, I put off needed conversations longer than I should. T or F
>
>   d. I avoid situations that bring me into contact with people that I have problems with. T or F
>
>   e. I don't give others negative feedback even when it's necessary. T or F
>
>   f. I change the subject when others bring up difficult or awkward subjects. T or F
>
>   If you marked "true" to two or more statements, you are an "avoider." Are you ready to change if *Navigating Conflict* gives you skills and strategies and shows you how to use them?
>
> 4. What in your work or home life would improve if you could figure out how to talk about "hot topics" without taking too much risk? What will you gain if you turn from a conflict "avoider" into a person willing to speak up?
>
> 5. Is there a small conflict in your work or home life that you could start on? Pick one or two. You don't need to tackle these issues immediately. Once you've read enough to gain confidence in using the skills, strategies, tactics, and tools you'll find in these pages, you'll be ready.
>
> 6. What do your answers to the first questions tell you?

CHAPTER 3

What Stops You From Handling Conflict?

You gain strength, courage, and confidence by every experience in which you really stop to look fear in the face. You must do the thing you think you cannot do.

—Eleanor Roosevelt

What stops you from handling conflict or from speaking up when you needed to?

Is it that:

☑ You're afraid if you speak up or try to fix things, you'll make the situation worse?

☑ You're afraid you'll make the other person angry and lose a relationship or job?

☑ You're afraid you'll say the wrong thing or otherwise stick your foot in your mouth?

☑ You're afraid the other person might retaliate?

☑ You fear that regardless of what you say, it won't make a positive difference?

☑ You're afraid to trigger an argument with someone who's adamant about getting their own way?

☑ You're afraid you'll be seen as uncaring, overly sensitive, or judgmental?

☑ You fear that if you start speaking, all the feelings you have pent up will explode?

☑ You acquiesce to keep the peace, fearing the alternative?

☑ You fear you might start a fight you can't win?

Have you noticed that every item listed includes an element of fear? Here's the truth:

You've magnified the risks of speaking up.

You've minimized the costs of not speaking up.

You've chosen to bite your tongue instead of believing your speaking up can achieve a good outcome. You don't speak up because you sense the other person holds all the power and might exact revenge. You fear the situation might blow up on you.

You'd rather live with the problem and let conflict lurk in the corners than voice your thoughts. You weigh your relationships and yourself down with unsaid words.

You may even play charades, thinking it easier to rely on nonverbal hints and subtle innuendoes to get your message across. Regrettably, you're not that good an actress/actor. Others rarely receive the message you hope they would. Instead, when you suppress your feelings, your frustration and anger simmer into a toxic brew that eats you up inside or bubbles up.

Perhaps you're a supervisor or manager who avoids addressing problem situations or employees but justifies your inaction to yourself, with statements, such as:

- ☑ "She's only two years from retirement."
- ☑ "Our department can't afford to lose him."
- ☑ "This situation might get better with time."
- ☑ "The results he achieves outweigh his attitude problems."
- ☑ "Everyone likes her and will take her side."

Here's the outcome of backing yourself into a self-justification corner. If you're a supervisor or manager who doesn't speak up, your team falters. The problem employee you don't address irritates others. Your other employees consider you a weak leader.

If you're an individual who doesn't speak up, your self-worth takes a hit, and you sentence yourself to living with the unresolved conflict.

If you feel it's time to take a risk, to marshal the courage, and speak up… read Chapter 4, Courage is Your Partner.

Your Turn: Action Steps

1. You can ready yourself to address a conflict by assessing it. There's no risk to this step; you can do this entire step in the privacy of your office, home, or in your head. Let's begin: What's a conflict you'd like to/need to address?

   a. Explain the conflict from your perspective:

   b. What sets it off?

   c. What feelings does the conflict/situation arouse in you?

   d. What makes the situation especially hard for you?

   e. What kind of relationship do you have with the other person?

   f. What kind of relationship do you want to have with the other person?

   g. What is your goal?

   h. How can you bring this conflict up?

   i. What stops you?

2. What did you learn from the assessment you just made? How many reasons stop you from addressing this conflict? Do you view them as reasons or excuses? What positive outcome might you gain from addressing this conflict?

CHAPTER 4

Courage Is Your Partner

Only those who will risk going too far can possibly find out how far one can go.

—T.S. Eliot

It takes courage to speak up, especially with someone who matters to you or who seems to have all the power. It's hard to voice your thoughts or needs when you see things differently than everyone else does.

In this chapter, you'll develop your partnership with courage. While individuals with courage may feel fear, they take a risk—and do or say what needs to be done or said. They conquer their hesitation and step outside their comfort zone.

If you currently back away from tackling conflict and need to marshal your courage, consider:

The Price of "Playing It safe"

When you face a choice between silence and the higher risk/greater reward alternative of speaking up, do you tell yourself "It's not so bad the way things are?" Do you imagine what might go wrong and let the potential consequences stop you? If so, you take a greater risk.

In your hesitation to travel outside your comfort zone, you forget that the real risk might be things staying the same and letting problems fester. You sell yourself out; underestimating your ability to handle what might happen.

If you have always traveled the road of silence, give thought to where it has led you. Six months from now, will you wish you'd trusted more in yourself?

Unlock the Power of Courage

What happens when you fear risk too much to move forward? Fear erodes confidence. Hesitation amplifies worry. If you allow fear to establish residence in your brain, fear not only moves in, it *owns* you.

What needs to happen for you to decide you'll actively handle conflict, even if right now the skills and strategies seem beyond your reach? In my earlier book, *Beating the Workplace Bully*, I wrote "think what a brave person would do, and become that brave person." The outcome you gain if you take this step is that you grow your courage by thinking your way through risk.

What If You Fail?

Here's how to never feel you've failed. Before you take a risk, consider the worst outcomes that might happen. Assess their likelihood and plan what you'll do if the worst happens and how you'll shift the odds for success in your favor. You've just lessened any risk.

Next, check your attitude. I remember meeting with a friend who started his own business the same month I launched mine. When he asked how I felt about having started my business, I said, "It's scary. I'm doing a lot of things I don't know how to do well. What's it like for you?"

His response came immediately. "It's exciting. I'm trying a lot of things I've never done before."

His answer changed my paradigm, reminding me I had a choice—excitement or fear. What about you? Is there a relatively safe but risky situation in which you need to speak up? Might you do it poorly or even fail? Or might you succeed?

When you try something new or take a risk and it doesn't work out, you learn. You grow wiser and better. Once you learn from your mistakes, you're no longer the same person who didn't know what you needed to understand to succeed. Viewed from this perspective, playing it safe doesn't make you more secure, it robs you of an opportunity to grow and leaves you less safe than before.

Taking small risks develops your conflict resolution muscles and teaches you to conquer your fear. You never fail when you try.

What's lost if you don't try? You live your life regretting the risks you didn't take, the times you didn't stand up for yourself, and the words you should have spoken but swallowed. As Wayne Gretzky once said, "You miss 100 percent of the shots you don't take." The bottom line: don't swap your backbone for a wishbone.

Your Turn: Action Steps

Now it's your turn. By answering the following questions, you may uncover goals, challenges, or insights valuable in the conflict coaching journey you've undertaken with this book. By answering these questions, you take the next step in authoring your life:

1. What are three (or more) talents you possess?
2. What are two accomplishments or successes you've had?
3. How have you improved during the past year?
4. What do you need to learn in the area of courage? What do you need to try?
5. What feelings or insights have you received from the first four chapters in *Navigating Conflict* or from answering the previous questions?
6. You might find it helpful to keep a conflict journal in which you record what you're learning. In it you can explain why certain situations hit you hard; where you feel vulnerable; what your feelings and reactions tell you; what knocks you off your feet or makes you uncomfortable, and above all, what you're discovering and how you're growing.

PART 2

Toughening Up

In these four chapters, you'll gain essential skills and tactics for:

- Handling yourself under fire
- Creating the "you" that stands up for yourself
- Skillfully handling criticism
- Developing an arsenal for counter-attacking attacking comments

CHAPTER 5

Learning to Handle Yourself Under Fire

The best way to make your dreams come true is to wake up.

—Paul Valery

Imagine two large, angry wolves, their teeth bared in ferocious snarls, circling you. You might freeze in fear and temporarily pause your breathing or breathe rapidly and shallowly. In the grip of your desire to flee or scream, you could lose the fight before it begins.

Now imagine you're verbally attacked by someone in a position of power, who seems to hold all the cards, or you're placed in a tense situation in which peace in your family or your job is on the line. While these problems don't pose the physical threat circling wolves do, you might react in the same way—your body tenses and your breathing halts.

If you've ever wondered why you often can't talk or think clearly in conflict situations, or why the response you should have said only occurs to you after you exit the situation; the answer lies in what you realized above and what you can learn to control: your breathing.

Here's what you need to understand. You have two hemispheres in your brain, left and right. Each controls different functions. The left hemisphere controls logic, analysis, linear thought, language, strategic thinking, and the sense of future consequences. The right hemisphere control reaction, emotion, intuition, and creativity.

When you breathe rapidly and shallowly, you momentarily lose easy, simultaneous access to both hemispheres. To successfully handle conflict, you need to be in touch with your feelings and also access language and problem-solving functions, enabling you to put your thoughts into words, determine an action, and consider the consequences of that action.

Fear, anxiety, or any emotional reactions pull you toward your right hemisphere. If you've ever been so upset you couldn't speak, it at least partially resulted because you lost temporary access to language which is housed in your left hemisphere. Similarly, you may have said or done things you later deeply regretted when reacting, in part because you temporarily lost access to your sense of future consequences. This phenomenon also explains why you can intuitively grasp another person's motivation yet be unable to use what you perceive in an analytical, problem-solving manner.

When you slow and deepen your breathing, you increase your ability to simultaneously access both left and right hemispheres. You can then partner analysis and problem solving with emotional and intuitive understanding.

Coastline Breathing

Here's a breathing technique you can immediately master. Imagine you're standing on a coast and gazing out at waves. Let yourself see them moving first toward and then away from shore. Does that image relax you?

Now, notice the path the air takes coming into and out of your body. You first inhale; then, there's a momentary pause, after which you exhale. You again momentarily pause prior to your next inhalation. The process resembles a wave-like pattern.

Now, close your eyes and notice your breathing process or flow in the same way you would watch waves. Allow yourself to relax with your breathing, letting it become slower and deeper. That's coastline breathing.

Now, with your eyes open, try it again and allow yourself to breathe in and out rhythmically. If this relaxes you, you've gained a tool you can use in any potentially tense situation.

Now let's test it out. Think of a person or situation that irritates you. Even as you think of that person or situation, allow yourself to slowly breathe. Notice the difference.

Controlling your initial instinctive reaction frees you to maintain your emotional balance and to respond rather than react.

Your Turn: Action Steps

1. Practice your coastline breathing in a variety of situations in the next two days—when you watch television, stand in line at the grocery store, or wait on hold on the phone. Practice it until it becomes second nature.

2. Write CB (for coastline breathing) on a sticky note and put it next to your computer monitor. Write it at the top of your legal pad before you go into a staff meeting. Notice that you can breathe deeply and slowly while listening to others or when you're getting ready to talk.

3. Teach at least one other person how to coastline breathe, because by teaching another person, you help yourself integrate how coastline breathing helps you in situations in which you formerly reacted.

CHAPTER 6

Creating the "You" Who Stands Up for Yourself

We must build dikes of courage to hold back the flood of fear.
—Martin Luther King Jr.

- ☑ *Do others manipulate you?*
- ☑ *Do you walk on eggshells around temperamental individuals?*
- ☑ *Do you quake inside when you consider standing up for yourself?*
- ☑ *Does someone in your work life or home life intimidate you— and know it?*
- ☑ *Do you go with the flow even when it takes you where you don't want to go?*

In terms of learning to handle conflict, you're poised, or maybe crouched, on the starting line. Although you may not be able to see the solid conflict resolution skills finish line because it's miles away, over that rushing river, through that tunnel, and over those hills—you can still reach it.

Let's start with the truth. Your past doesn't predict your future unless *you* bring your past with you. Also, a lot of what you need to conquer lies in your head. Anything that gets in your way of handling conflict needs to be examined. Is it fear, the sense you don't deserve better, or because you feel you can't be honest and at the same time diplomatic? Let's explore how your mental baggage gets in your way.

The Impact of What's in Your Mind

Mental experiment #1: Imagine you're asked to walk the length of an eight-foot-long two-by-four plank laid on the ground. You can do it.

Let yourself see yourself doing it in your mind by imagining laying a plank down in the largest room in your house and walking its length. Easy.

Now imagine your friend lifts that plank up three inches off the ground, stabilizes it on both ends, and offers you $5.00 if you walk across its length.

You look at the plank, realize it's only three inches off the ground, and decide very little could go wrong. You accept the challenge and smile as you hold out your hand for the $5.00.

But what happens if your friend raises the plank 10 feet off the ground and stabilizes it on both ends—would you walk its length now? Would you see it as too great a risk, even though you walked it easily when was lying on the ground?

What got in the way? If you answer that it was fear that's housed in your mind, you answered correctly.

Mental experiment #2: Please stand, taking this book with you, and notice the location of your feet. Now, leave your feet in that same position, turn your entire body to the right or the left without moving your feet, and notice the furthest spot on the wall you can see. Memorize that spot.

Next, leaving your feet in the same position, memorize the following instructions, and lay the book down. Once you've done that, close your eyes while imagining an empowering, relaxing light descending around your head. Allow yourself to feel this relaxing light energy massaging the back and sides of your head and neck. Let yourself feel your neck becoming more supple, flexible, and malleable.

Continue imagining this empowering, relaxing energy descending, massaging your shoulders, upper ribs, and back. Allow yourself to feel your back and shoulders growing looser, more at ease, and more limber.

Now with your feet in the same place as earlier, open your eyes, turn your entire body without moving your feet, and notice the furthest spot on the wall you see. You'll likely see further. If that happens, you've experienced the power your mind has.

Let's go further. Have you ever heard that "acting as if" you feel confident strengthens you from the inside out? Here's an example that shows you the truth of this statement.

Please stand or sit as if you're depressed. You'll likely feel your shoulders slump, your head tilt down, and your chest cave inward. Now, maintain that stance while letting yourself feel powerful, joyous, enthusiastic, and excited. If you're like most people, these positive words made you want to stand or sit taller and straighter.

Now, stand or sit as if something wonderful has happened. Chances are you'll stand or sit straight and tall, looking forward with a smile lighting your face. Allow your smile to beam, and then, without losing your posture or changing your facial expression, let yourself feel fearful, humiliated, embarrassed, intimidated, or depressed. Do you find it hard to do?

You've just learned that how or what you feel impacts how you stand or sit.

Experiment #4: Similarly, how you stand or sit impacts what you feel inside, which is why so many people suggest you act "as if" you're confident even when you're not.

To really understand this, try this experiment. Please sit like a well-mannered lady (even you guys), with your ankles crossed and hands folded in your lap. Could you possibly take up any less space? Do you feel submissive in this position?

Now, sit like a confident, secure, assertive individual. You immediately take up more space even though your body size doesn't change. How does this shift in position impact you? Do you feel more ready to handle what might come at you? If so, the next time someone confronts you and your body assumes a submissive posture, remember to sit up, straighten your back and shoulders, and assume a more confident position.

Mental Martial Arts

Visualization gives you an additional tool that empowers you when you face a challenge or need to relax.

To learn how this tool works, close your eyes and visualize one of your children or pets in an adorable moment. Or imagine a peaceful natural scene such as a beach, waterfall, mountain meadow, or sailboat floating calmly out to sea. Do you feel your body relaxing?

Now, think of someone who intimidates or rubs you the wrong way. Imagine them on a stage in front of you saying or doing things you don't like. As you see this short scene play in your mind's eye, you might notice that your breathing pauses, your shoulders tighten, your face flushes, or your palms start to sweat.

Now, try this experiment. Let yourself see the irritating scene play out while at the same time envisioning the face of your adorable child or puppy or a special place in nature that you find peaceful and relaxing. Do you notice how the image you mentally flash on shifts your energy or changes how you feel?

You now have a tool you can use in any encounter. Here's why it works. Mentally flashing on a relaxing scene or beloved face centers or grounds you. You can focus on it even as you remain fully aware of what's going on around you because the mental flash is visual, and visual processing moves at the equivalent rate of 900 to 1,400 words per minute. Because spoken words process at the rate of 80 to 180 words per minute, you can multitask, mentally flashing on an image while hearing every word the other person speaks. You can even flash on an image while you're talking. Try it.

You can use this same multitasking technique with other images to strengthen yourself. Bring into your mind the image of a strong actress or actor (such as Meryl Streep, Sandra Bullock, Katharine Hepburn, Clint Eastwood, John Wayne, or Denzel Washington) with their head held high. Alternatively, let yourself see a majestic mountain, such as Denali or Everest in your mind, and imagine yourself drawing strength from the mountain. Notice the feeling of strength you sense as you mentally flash on these strong faces or those mountains.

Mental Kevlar

Please look at the following list of words. Which ones describe you?

Honest
Caring
Generous
Kind
Loyal
Compassionate
Responsible

Funny

Genuine

Curious

Enthusiastic

Adventurous

Fair

Natural

Imaginative

Understanding

Intuitive

Perceptive

Good-hearted

Open-minded

Fun-loving

Creative

Resourceful

Trustworthy

Helpful

Friendly

Kind

Cheerful

Brave

How many?—5, 10, 15? All 23? If even five of these words fit you, you possess admirable qualities. Have you let another person brainwash you into forgetting that? Have you forgotten your good qualities because you've been kicking yourself for a situation you've gotten yourself into?

Next, create a list of five additional positive words that describe you. If they're slow to come to mind, think of some of the words your friends or those who look up to and respect you would say when describing your best qualities. Once you've created this list, re-read your list and the items checked on the previous list. Would you want a friend who has the positive qualities you've listed? Of course. You have those qualities and it's time you honored the person you are. The next day someone nasty tries to hitch a ride in your head by making mean comments to you, tell them, "This car's full," because it is, with the positives you know are true of you.

Let's add depth to your Kevlar. Take a moment to think of two challenges you handled well or at least survived. What do these experiences tell you about your strength and resilience?

The next time you're tempted to overly criticize yourself for mistakes you've made, remember these challenges you're handled. Isn't it time you became your best cheerleader rather than your worst critic?

Reprogramming Your Mental Tapes Concerning You and Conflict

Most of us have one or more destructive mental tapes depicting how we handle conflict. You may consider yourself a weak person who lets yourself be walked on. You may curse your instinct to impulsively say the wrong words and make a difficult situation worse. Or perhaps you have another conflict resolution weakness that rises to the surface when you face conflict.

The "change your mental tape" strategy helps you nuke any self-doubting statements that impede your standing up for yourself. Pick any statement or "tape" you tell yourself that weakens you, for example, "I'll never learn to stand up for myself" or "Other people can take advantage of me because they're smarter than I am."

You can dismantle a tape like this by repeating it four times against a changing mental background until it loses all or much of the power it holds over you. Imagine that you have a tape recorder in your mind with six buttons on the front of it. Press button one and hear whatever statement or "tape" you've selected play softly in your mind. Hear it said again, this time loudly.

Press button two and hear that statement said very s-l-o-w-l-y. Then, hear it said very quickly as if recorded at hyper speed.

Press button three and hear the statement with merry-go-round music playing in the background. Hear it again accompanied by Wagnerian music such as the "Ride of the Valkyries," with cymbals clanging and drums banging. Hear it one final time as if Donald Duck, Bugs Bunny, or another cartoon character with a funny voice might say it. Has it become harder to take this "tape" seriously?

Now, press the sixth and final button marked "new tape" on the right front of the tape recorder. Create an affirmative statement and let yourself hear it as if spoken out loud. You might select a statement such as "I show courage" or "I am determined to live the life I want." Hear this statement said again and again in a clear, firm, positive voice. How does it make your feel? Does the earlier negative statement have as much power as this newer tape? Or does the new statement more engage your mind?

What does this teach you? You can uproot any negative statement that's damaged your heart or spirit using the mental tape recorder strategy.

Mental Resolve

Deciding *what* is important to stand up for helps you develop the "you" that stands up for yourself. Let's do this for real. Please select a current conflict in your life. What's going on? Is this how you want to be treated? Is this situation worth taking on?

What do you gain from answering these three questions? If you sense that you gain an increased desire to stand up for yourself, you've learned the use of a new tool.

Changing Your Habits

In this chapter, you've received many insights and learned a variety of new skills and strategies that you might want to adopt as new habits. Here's what you can expect when you try to make these changes—your brain will work with you. When you try out a new habit or behavior, your mind automatically creates a new neurological pathway to support the habit. Each time you repeat the habit, your thoughts travel across this new neural pathway.

As your thoughts more frequently travel across this new mental pathway, it becomes the route more likely for your thoughts to instinctively travel. Repeat a new habit for 8–21 days, even with occasional relapses, until your new habit takes over the earlier pattern. This practice means the more often you handle conflict in new ways, the more those patterns become yours.

Your Turn: Action Steps

1. While your past doesn't predict your future unless you bring your past with you, you often lug your past along unless you consciously decide how you want to change. What do you want to change about how you approach conflict?

2. Create two powerful images that help you center yourself and practice visualizing them while interacting with others.

3. For the next two days, notice your posture. Do you stand tall? Or do you shrink?

4. Choose one of the experiments you tried in this chapter and teach it to a friend or loved one. You may notice that you gain even more from the experiment when you teach it to someone else and notice their eyes lighting up as they learn something new.

5. Repeat the task given in the last two paragraphs of this chapter. Select a current conflict in your life and this time write about it. What's going on? Is this how you want to be treated? What changes do you want to see made—by you, and then by the other person. Is this situation worth addressing? What's the first step you can take to address this conflict?

6. What are the two important insights you've taken away from reading this chapter and doing these exercises that you'll want to remember and use?

CHAPTER 7

Teflon Yourself to Criticism

Which of the following eight situations fits you?

1. Your workplace or family life resembles an episode of Survivor, and only those with thick armor on their emotional skin escape as whole.
2. You live or work with one or more individuals who see every one of your flaws and don't hesitate to tell you about them.
3. After you've tried your best in a difficult situation, your manager flattens you by saying "not good enough." Or perhaps your significant other or teenager judges you daily and lets you know you come up short.
4. A co-worker or friend upon whose opinion you count on treats you with disrespect. Then, when you ask for their honest thoughts, they say things that cut you to the core.
5. You work under a supervisor who consistently tears apart the work you turn in. Or perhaps your parent regularly criticizes the decisions you've made or how you live your life.
6. You don't mind valid criticism but are criticized by individuals who don't know what they're talking about.
7. One of your critic's comments—that you don't take criticism well—irritates you because you can't defend against it. If you disagree, you prove their point.
8. You're your own worst critic.

If several of these situations fit you, you face criticism challenges. In fact, no matter how hard you try or how good you are, you can expect criticism, particularly in conflict situations. Sometimes you're ready for it. Sometimes it blindsides you. Sometimes it hobbles your attempts to handle the conflict.

If you'd like to turn being criticized—whether by your manager, co-workers, loved ones, or yourself—to your benefit, here's how:

Pause Before You Respond

When you're criticized, your instincts take over. You might immediately defend yourself by saying "that's not true," by justifying your actions or by offering excuses. You might throw criticisms of your own at the critic or attack their right to criticize you.

None of these reactions produces positive results. When you attack back, it increases the criticism's shelf life and builds a wall between you and the other person. When you react defensively, you deny problems or issues, leaving them unsolved and festering. Worse, you establish yourself to others as defensive and fail to learn information that could help you improve.

Counter your instinctive reaction by training yourself to pause before you react. By pausing, you short-circuit your defensive reaction, hear what was said, and give yourself the chance to respond wisely.

Choose a Proactive Response

You have three proactive choices for responding to criticism. If someone says, "You didn't listen to me," you can say "I'm sorry" (agreeing), "I've heard enough" (disagreeing), or ask "What did I miss?" (questioning). Asking a question often works best because it gives you control of the interaction and moves you and your critic toward a solution.

Agreeing Can Evaporate the Criticism and Move You and the Critic Forward

If you receive accurate criticism, your best choice may be to accept the criticism. If a manger or co-worker points out errors you missed in a report you filed, take another look at the report. If the criticism is valid, admit it and make the corrections.

If your significant other gets upset because you were late to an event, left things in a mess, or made statements you already regret, admit you messed up and apologize.

If your boss says, "You could and should have done a better job," show your maturity and willingness to grow by responding, "Thanks, I learned from what you said; here's what I'll do differently next time," or "Here's what I'll do to fix this."

If your teenager or child tells you that you hurt their feelings or let them down, apologize. By acknowledging legitimate criticism you take much of the air out of a ballooning problem.

Agreeing with accurate criticism doesn't mean you accept others' opinions without thinking; rather it moves you through the criticism to a productive solution. Agreement comes from a powerful source—your intent to accept responsibility and move forward.

Agreeing doesn't include making the criticism bigger or holding on to it. If your supervisor tells you to improve your work performance, don't dive off the deep end and turn in your resignation. If a friend says you let him or her down, don't refuse to speak with him or her for a week. Assess what was said without magnifying it and identify how you can improve. There's no benefit to holding onto criticism once you've heard it. Learn, change, and move on.

You Have the Right to Disagree

You have as much right to evaluate your behavior as your critic. If someone criticizes you inaccurately, say so. If a co-worker says, "You should have gone to that meeting," and you disagree, you can respond, "I evaluated the agenda and decided against attending."

If your teenager says, "You should let me do this because Joe's parents allowed it," you can respond, "I don't feel comfortable allowing it." When you disagree with inaccurate criticism, a simple "I don't agree" or a brief explanation is more convincing than a lengthy defense.

Ask a Question

We often react to criticism so quickly we don't learn from it. If someone says, "You're irritating," and you argue "I'm not" or attack with "You're the one who's irritating," you shut off dialogue and potential improvement. If you instead ask, "What did I do that irritated you?" you open up a discussion that can resolve the situation and lead to an improved relationship.

Further, if the other person attacked you unfairly, your proactive questioning moves the responsibility of explaining onto them. If your critic is a sniper or bully, by asking a question you establish control over the interaction. Instead of the other's criticism knee-capping you, knocking you off balance, and less able to handle the situation, you gain the upper hand.

If asking questions works, why don't more of us do it? It's likely that we fear opening the conversational door to the critic. Yet, by opening that door, we give ourselves the chance to hear and improve, thus disarming our critics and resolving problems.

Turn a Critic Into Your Coach

If your critic is your manager, spouse, or significant other, you share a mutual goal—improving you. You can make that goal a reality by thanking the other person, saying you want to improve and then asking what he or she recommends you do to improve yourself or the situation.

This situation happened to me with a prospect during my first month in business as a management consultant. I met with Jack, a senior manager at Atlantic Richfield Company, and presented my training programs. He said, "You seem dynamic, but you're not the right fit for our managers."

I responded, "I'd like to be. But more than that, I'd like to know how I don't measure up. Could you give me ten minutes of coaching?" He gave me an hour, and we stayed in regular contact for three years. I let him know I planned to visit Alyeska Pipeline Service Company later that week and when I arrived there, I learned that Jack had called ahead, told them I had a lot of guts and charisma, and suggested they take a chance on my training to train their field technicians. Jack later gave me multiple opportunities to train managers, supervisors, and front-line staff at Atlantic Richfield and the company remained a solid client for decades. You can turn criticism and rejection into a golden opportunity.

You have the same opportunity with family, friends, and loved ones. Don't squander it.

Seize Every Learning Opportunity

If you're your own worst critic, turn that criticism habit into a growth initiator. In the chapter on courage, I admitted how a friend said starting a new business was exciting right after I described starting a new business as scary. Instead of criticizing myself for admitting fear, I used the conversational wake-up call to shift my paradigm.

Self-criticism can either disenable or inspire you. When you criticize yourself, you tell yourself where and how you need to improve. That's great inspiration. Act on it.

Meanwhile, if you're your own worst critic, cut yourself some slack concerning the problem habits you have that get on your nerves. For example, if you're like me and thrifty, you don't always buy what appeals to you, reasoning "Maybe I don't need it." Later, when you regret what you didn't buy and go back to make the purchase, you may find the item isn't available.

You can kick yourself or give yourself credit. Yes, your thriftiness cost you something you wanted, but it has saved thousands of dollars over the years and on balance has worked to your benefit.

Your Turn: Action Steps

It can be a challenge to respond positively and professionally to criticism in the moment and without first practicing. Exercise one and two give you that practice. Exercise three powers your growth in turning self-criticism to your advantage.

1. Write down three criticisms that others have given you. Read each out loud to yourself and respond, using each of the three options: agree; disagree, or ask a question. Remember to pause before you respond. For example, if I wrote, "You could have handled your ex-husband better," I could respond (a) "I could have," (b) "I don't think so," or (c) "What could I have done differently?"
   When you do this practice notice which option comes easiest to you and whether you're tempted to justify yourself or to attack the criticism. Practice until you get good at this.
2. Imagine each of the following criticisms is directed toward you. When you hear each said in your mind, take a calming breath and ask a question.
   a. You're too sensitive.

(*Continues*)

(Continued)

> b. You always overreact.
>
> c. You shouldn't be so emotional.
>
> d. You can't take a joke.
>
> e. You have no sense of humor.
>
> What did you learn from this practice? (*By the way, learning to respond with a question gets easier over time.*)
>
> 3. Write down any criticisms you get in the coming weeks and practice responding by pausing and trying out each of the three options. Congratulate yourself when pausing and asking questions becomes your second nature.
>
> 4. Keep an insights journal. Life is your proving ground and you'll experience multiple times in the next weeks and months when you make mistakes for which you criticize yourself. Consider what you learn from each of these situations and write down promises to yourself for what you'll do differently.

CHAPTER 8

Develop Your Arsenal for Counteracting Attacking Comments

In Chapter 7, you learned to handle criticism so you could learn from and not be flattened by it. In this chapter, you'll further develop your skills by:

- ☑ Learning to handle verbal jabs, snipes, and attacks that formerly left you tongue-tied or defensive
- ☑ Building an arsenal of responses that neutralize attacking comments
- ☑ Learning an easy-to-implement strategy for turning the tables on a verbal attacker

Winning the Inside Game

Verbal jabs, snipes, and attacks can leave you rattled, embarrassed, tongue-tied, and defensive. An attacking barrage can twist you into emotional and mental knots and chip away at your sense of self. Verbal attackers focus their and your attention on anything negative, reducing your self-confidence and making you more susceptive to manipulation and control.

Each attack sets a game in motion. Don't play this game; don't let the attacker's rude comments plunge you into self-doubt and rule the day.

You've already learned two key skills for overturning the negative game board: breathing and alternate focus. Breathing enables you to gather your thoughts and allows you to link language, creativity, and problem-solving skills. Alternate focus or the mental "flash" strategy helps you ground and center yourself.

Building Your Arsenal

When you create an arsenal of memorized statements, you add a powerful tool that neutralizes verbal attacks.

Imagine that you are talking with a friend and a third party inserts themself into your conversation and makes a caustic comment about what you just said. You ask, "Pardon me?" with a warm, neutral expression on your face as if you can't imagine the other person meant to say what they said.

What happens? While this person might repeat the comment, you've established that they can't simply jab at you without you handling it. If the commenter does repeat the comment, or even escalates, you can respond, "Got it." Although you neither reacted defensively nor attacked them, you've put up a wall that says you don't appreciate that type of snark.

Imagine you're in a staff meeting and you've presented a proposal, and another team member slams what you've offered by saying, "that proposal isn't even worth the time it would take to discuss it," effectively shutting down anyone who might positively comment on your proposal.

Two can play the crowd game. If you say, "If that statement is all you have to offer, I'd like others to weigh in," you take the upper hand and invite others for their comments. This response both restarts the discussion and makes it easier for others to provide positive comments.

Your arsenal might include the following:

A calm "your point?" which says you don't think there was one.

"Give it a rest" or "game over," which says you're done being attacked.

"Nice try," "nice bait," or "I don't think so," all indicate you're aware your attacker tried to derail or wound you but failed.

Whenever you're responding, remember to breathe first and speak in a calm tone that signals your attacker's missile hasn't penetrated.

If your attacker persists, you can say, "Lay it on me; take your best shot." Notice what happens internally when you say this. You've told yourself as well as your attacker that you can handle them.

You can follow up any of these arsenal statements with a stronger comeback. If in response to "pardon me?" your attacker escalates with "Do you have a problem with your hearing?" you can respond, "No. I wanted to give you a chance to remove your foot from your mouth."

If the verbal attacker smirks and says, "Just kidding," or "Why are you making a big deal about this?" thus blaming you for feeling stung, you can say, "I'm not okay with disrespect."

The bottom line—you don't let others disrespect you and you do so in a way that isn't defensive or attacking.

Turning the Tables With a Question

If I verbally attack you, and you get defensive, who has the stronger position? I do.

If I attack you with an angry comment, and you angrily comment back, who has the upper hand? I do. I pushed your buttons and you reacted.

If I verbally attack and you ask a question, who now controls the interaction? You do.

As you learned in the earlier chapter on handling criticism, training yourself to respond with questions protects you in a way that neither retaliating nor defending does.

Here's a workplace example. Assume I'm your supervisor and yell at you, "Is that all you got done?" and you respond, "I'm sorry it took so long," I've placed you on the apologetic defensive. If you angrily respond, "You have no clue how much effort this took," you're still playing my game. If, however, you ask "What would you like me to work on next?" using a professional tone, you take over the lead position, forcing me to answer your question.

Imagine one of your peers asks, "Where'd you come up with this crap?" when you share what you've produced thus far on a joint assignment. Regardless of how you answer, you may appear to be defending what you've created. If you instead ask, "What are you getting at?" you turn the tables.

What if one of the younger members in your family insults you with "You're an irritating old fool!" Countering with, "You're the irritating one," or "I'm not," accomplishes little. If you instead ask, "What exactly do you find irritating?" you seize control of the interaction and start a dialog.

Once you learn to ask a question whenever someone snipes or jabs at you, you can have fun. Imagine the reaction if someone says to you, "You look like a dog," and you respond with "what breed?" You've just announced, "I'm immune" to nasty comments and "you'd better be prepared to explain yourself." If the verbal sniper attacked you in front of an audience, they'll laugh with and not at you.

Let's assume one of your employees says, "you're the worst supervisor ever," and you respond with "what do you want me to change?" You've just thrown the responsibility back to your employee.

Perhaps one of your holier-than-thou employees accuses you by saying, "You're so confusing; you've lost me" when you give an assignment. By asking, "Where'd I lose you?" you make the employee's statement a problem to be solved and short-circuit the underlying blaming message. If your employee answers, "Right at the beginning," and you respond by repeating what you've already said, you'll let employee learn that their reward for the "confusing" attack is hearing the assignment repeated.

Questions also help you avoid the "yes/no" trap. If your attacker says, "Do you cut your own hair?" implying with their tone that you have a lousy haircut, and you ask, "What makes that important to you?" you take the upper hand.

Your Turn: Action Steps

1. Practice saying statements, such as "I'm not playing," "Nonsense," "Nice bait," and "Game over." If you have a dog or cat, use these statements with them when your animal pushes you too far—it's good practice.

2. Has a verbal attacker hammered away at your vulnerabilities? How did you handle it? What have you now learned that you can do instead?

3. Spend an hour and build your arsenal of neutralizing statements. Feel free to borrow every example provided in this chapter.

4. Think back to a verbal attack you've received. If you haven't recently received one, make one up. What "game over" response could you have given?

5. When you're next verbally attacked, and it's politic for you to handle it differently, consider it an opportunity for practice. Choose one of the statements you've practiced that fits the situation, such as "No, I don't accept that."

   How did it work? If it worked well, congratulate yourself and enjoy the fact that you're growing less likely to be derailed or flattened by verbal attacks. If it didn't work as well as you hoped, what did you learn and what will you do better the next time?

6. Practice responding to the following attacking statements with questions:
   - Where did you come up with this crap?
   - You are impossibly dumb.
   - You're a bitch.
   - Can't you ever do anything right?
   - How could you be so stupid?
   - You moron.
   - You really made a mess of that.
   - You're a fat cow.

7. Is there someone in your work or personal life who tries to control you with verbal attacks? What have you learned in this chapter that can help you stop them?

PART 3

Your Tool Chest

Skills and Tactics for Defusing 75 Percent of Conflicts

In the next four chapters, you'll learn:

- ☑ How to listen in way that convinces the other person you've heard and ensures you won't miss crucial information.
- ☑ How to get any other person comfortable with you and how to know when you've succeeded.
- ☑ How to question another in a way that surfaces key issues without offending or pushing buttons.
- ☑ How to bring up issues so they can be resolved.

CHAPTER 9

Listening As If You Mean It

In this chapter, you'll learn, or perhaps relearn, how to listen in a way that convinces the other person you've heard. Through listening, you build rapport, show respect, prevent misunderstanding, and de-escalate conflict. If you're involved in a brewing conflict, you gain crucial information you may need to resolve the conflict.

Here's the Truth

It's easy to give an excuse for not listening. You have other priorities and don't have time. The speaker rambles or bores you. You already know what you're about to hear.

It's harder to admit you're a poor listener—isn't listening something you do naturally?

No.

The opposite often proves true. You may find it hard to listen to someone who has something to say you don't want to hear. You may interrupt or tune out. Sometimes even when you wait until the speaker finishes, your brain remains focused on what you wanted to say in the first place.

The result—you miss hearing information you later wish you'd heard, or you may fall into "yes ... but" arguments in which neither you nor the other person comes to terms with each other's viewpoint. You also sacrifice opportunities to draw out the feelings and ideas of the other person. You then miss an opportunity, as listening can prevent future problems and lead the other person to be more likely to listen to you.

Often, the smartest people listen poorly. You may be one of them. Because you think quickly, you may have developed a listening pattern in which you interrupt frequently, causing others to feel unheard and shut out. As a result, others won't believe you care about what they have to say, or them as people, creating a breeding ground for conflict.

If you want to improve your listening skills, give the speaker your full attention. It's difficult to listen fully when thinking about what you want to say in response or keeping an eye on your computer monitor or cellphone. Even if you can listen while dual focusing, the other person may feel unheard. In your effort to do two things at once, you waste your time and the other person's time because the speaker feels shortchanged. If you genuinely pay attention even if you think you know what the other person may say, you can have conversations that explore real issues. If not, you may limit yourself to shallow, alternating monologs.

To help you accomplish this, develop the habit of paraphrasing or summarizing in your own words what the other person says. Paraphrasing means restating in your own words what you hear to make sure you've got it. Paraphrasing is *not* parroting, in which you restate exactly what the speaker said. Parroting can feel robotic to you and the other person.

Paraphrasing provides four benefits. 1) It FORCES you to listen; 2) clarifies what you've heard; 3) shows the speaker you've heard, and 4) reduces misunderstanding. For example, if your speaker says, "This situation makes me feel so frustrated because neither you nor Roberta gave me a chance to respond," you might ask, "So I upset you when I didn't give you an opening to say what you wanted?"

The speaker might then say, "Yes! Anyone would have been upset;" or "No, not upset, I didn't think you were being fair." With this example, you can already see how paraphrasing created a dialog that provided useful information.

When you paraphrase, most conversations improve. Without paraphrasing, two individuals in conflict move quickly into "yes ... but" arguments. With paraphrasing, you stay on the other person's wavelength and more easily reach the real issues of concern.

You can paraphrase more than the spoken word. If what the speaker leaves unsaid appears more important than what they said, or if you pick up on nonverbal clues, feel free to include them in your summary by making comments, such as, "It looks like I've caught you off guard." By paraphrasing perceptions, conversations move to deeper and more honest levels.

Listening—a communication and conflict resolution tool so commonplace you do it without thinking and forget to do it without noticing.

Your Turn: Action Steps

1. What listening habits do you have that make it difficult for you to honestly listen?
2. In the next several days, find as many opportunities as you can to paraphrase another person in casual conversation. Notice the effect. If you don't have many actual conversations that might give you a chance to paraphrase, practice paraphrasing what an actor or actress in a movie or television show says.
3. In the next week, select a person important to you and paraphrase what they say. Again, notice the effect.

CHAPTER 10

The Rapport Tool

Have you ever noticed how often you yawn, smile, or begin to drawl when you're talking with someone who yawns in front of you, smiles at you, or drawls when talking with you? In this chapter, you'll learn:

- Why unconscious mirroring or matching happens.
- Why some people don't match you.
- What nonverbal matching tells you is happening.
- How to use matching.
- What happens when you and another person don't match.

Matching Defined

When two people match, it means that they adopt similar nonverbal gestures, postures, or facial expressions. Matching can be identical, as it happens when another person smiles at you, and you smile back, or you may "crossmatch."

Crossmatching occurs when you mirror another person but match with different parts of your body, as when a woman crosses her legs and the man with her crosses his arms. Another form of crossmatching occurs when you nod your head in rhythm with someone who talks with a choppy speaking pattern.

Why We Match

We match or mirror out of a desire to be understood and liked. When we're with another person, we unconsciously adopt the other person's nonverbal behaviors and persona so they'll sense our similarity to them and as a result, will like us.

When People Don't Match Each Other

We don't match people we instinctively resist; those we dislike or distrust, or those from whom we feel different. This resistance happens within the first two minutes of interacting with another person. When we sense we're different from another, or instinctively distrust or feel uncomfortable with the other person, we unconsciously adopt a body position that reveals this underlying feeling. For example, if you're with a salesperson leaning toward you and forcefully attempting to sell you a product, you might lean back and away or even move backward a step.

Two other reasons for not mirroring exist. Individuals with poor communication and rapport skills don't match others. Individuals planning to tell a lie often mismatch in the seconds before their lie. Here's why. When we match, we feel rapport. Individuals who intend to lie often break away from that feeling of rapport by physically altering their posture prior to lying.

The Clues Matching Gives You

Matching offers you a window into how another person feels about you. When someone feels similar to or comfortable with you, or trusts you, matching happens.

Conversely, if someone doesn't feel comfortable with or trust you, or feels resistant to you or what you're saying, they won't match with you. You can see this result when a smiling person meets someone who's not happy with the situation. The unhappy person's face deepens its frown. You also see this reaction when an intense parent asks a teen, "how was school today?" and the teen becomes increasingly monotone and shuts down.

Matching thus offers you a litmus test for what isn't said. For example, imagine you have criticized another person, and they say they agree. If their body positioning doesn't mirror yours, they don't really accept your criticism. If, however, the person you criticize reacts defensively and tells you that you're wrong, but matches you; then, your words have reached them.

Matching As a Tool

You can use matching to create a sense of rapport and similarity between you and another.

For example, imagine you're an exuberant, fast-talking individual. You move into an interaction with an individual who's more subdued and slower in tempo. If you're paying attention, you'll take a deep breath, rein in your exuberance, and slow your talking pace. While you might think you can transmit your excitement to the other person by maintaining your exuberant animation, the opposite more often proves true. Your exuberance can cause others to shut down.

Here's a real-life example. When Fritz walks into Bill's office, he notices that Bill immediately adopts a defensive posture. Instead of critiquing Bill for his defensiveness, Fritz considers his own body language. He had barreled through the door, his arms wide with excitement. Immediately he stopped and retreated to stand in the doorframe, and asked, "Do you mind if I come in?" By modifying his approach, Fritz potentially achieved a better outcome.

Your Takeaway

Here's your takeaway. You don't need to worry if you and another person instinctively match each other. If you and another person don't instinctively match, it may be worth your effort to see if you can comfortably match the other person's posture or facial expressions.

Your Turn: Action Steps

1. Where have you noticed matching?
2. How do you sense that you can use matching?
3. Are there people to whom you instinctively mismatch? Try an experiment and force yourself to match to them. You may find this adjustment makes you uncomfortable. This feeling gives you an indication of how we do not want to match to those we don't like or trust.
4. In the next several days, practice matching those to whom you interact with until you become comfortable with observing nonverbal clues and using what you notice to increase your degree of matching.

CHAPTER 11

Conflict-Resolution Questions

How to Effectively Question to Surface Key Issues Without Offending or Pushing Buttons

If we could resolve conflicts using what we already know, life might be simpler. Unfortunately, resolving most conflicts requires you to learn and understand another's viewpoints. You do this by asking questions and listening to the other's answers.

Asking questions in a manner that doesn't make the other person feel defensive or attacked and that reveals what the other person truly thinks becomes critically important in resolving conflict. If you push buttons or offend another person as you question them, you won't learn what you need. The other person might shut down, tell you what they think you want to hear, or even give you information to mislead you.

Questions That Work

Four types of questions work well for resolving conflict:

- Open-ended
- Clarifying
- Narrowing
- Directional

Open-ended questions start with "what," "how," and "tell me more," and invite the other person in the conflict to explain their views. As an example, you might ask the other person, "How would you like us to work together?" "What do you want to have happen here?" "What would it take for us to move forward?" and "How do you see the situation differently?"

You can also use other words that start an open dialog such as, "Can you help me understand your thinking?" and "Can I ask how you saw the situation?"

Clarifying questions ensure you've understood what you've heard, because you and the other person may interpret words differently. These questions also help you look below the surface of what is first said by the other person.

For example, the other person may say, "We need to work as a team." For you, the "team" concept might mean a U.S. Olympic swim team in which team members perform in solo fashion although they all represent the same country. The other person may have in mind a soccer or a hockey team in which everyone plays an interconnected part.

Initially you might follow up with another open-ended question, "What does team mean to you?" The other person might answer, "Team means we help and support each other." You can then ask a clarifying question, such as, "What does help and support your fellow team members mean?"

Some open-ended questions also clarify another's views such as, "What will it take for you to let go of this?" and "What will it take for you to feel this has been resolved?"

Narrowing questions serve two purposes. First, they allow you to guide the conversation, such as when a clothing store salesperson asks, "Were you looking for a shirt in a color like as red or blue or were you looking for a white shirt?"

If you ask another person, "Are you hoping we meet tomorrow or would next week be better?" you give the other person several choices, all of which feel comfortable to you. If you ask, "When would you like to meet?" and the other person answers "today," you might find yourself having to say, "but I can't."

Narrowing questions also prove helpful when the other person finds it difficult to explain their thoughts. Then, by providing the other person two different alternatives, you help them choose one over the other, as you both work to narrow in on what the person means.

Directional questioning causes the other person to think in the direction in which you want them to proceed. For example, by asking, "What do you see as the benefits to our resolving this conflict?" you lead the other person to think of the benefits.

Question Types That Don't Work

Closed-ended and **leading** questions have limitations. Close-ended questions force a "yes" or a "no" and provide little information. Leading questions force an answer and often result in the other person shutting down because they don't want to give the answer you're pushing for. A question that's both close-ended and leading might be "Do you agree with me?"

The Word You Choose to Start the Question

Many of us begin questions with two words that interfere with our learning what we need to, such as "why" and "did."

Why

Notice how you react to the following questions that seek the same information but start with different words:

"Why did you say that?"
"Please tell me what led you to say that."
"Why do you think that?"
"What are your reasons?"
"Why did you quit your job?"
"What led to your decision to quit?"

What do you notice about the difference between the questions that start with "why" and the others?

"Why" can place the other person on the defensive.

Did

Similarly, "did" can negatively impact rapport, come across as parental, and leads to shorter answers. Compare the following:

"Did you clean your room?"
"Have you finished your room?"
"Did you finish the project?"
"What's the status on the project?"

Words That Serve as Effective for Starting Questions

Words, such as "what," "how," "tell me more," and "could you discuss (or share or explain)" prove more effective than "why" and "did" for starting questions.

Signal Words

When you truly listen, you'll hear "signal" words that signify valuable information lurking below the surface. You can then ask questions that delve deeper. For example, what jumps out at you if a team member says, "I want to start new initiatives and work on them from start to finish. I'd get a charge out of doing that." The speaker appears to have something in mind, and you might ask, "Is there a new initiative you have in mind?"

Your Turn: Action Steps

For the next two weeks, practice avoiding the words "why" and "did." You'll soon realize how often one or both words creep into your discussions.

1. Choose two different people that you'd like to get to know better and use your open-ended questioning skills on each of them. What benefits do you realize?
2. If your tendency is to listen silently to another person and assume you understand what the other person means, ask a clarifying question. Notice the benefits you achieve.

3. If there's someone in your home or work life that you hope starts to do or see things differently, create two directional questions. Select one of them and use it with the other person.

4. Ask yourself a series of directional questions, such as the following:

   a. What have you learned in this chapter you find useful? (This question reminds you to focus on your learning.)

   b. How does what you've learned benefit you? (This question focuses you on the benefits you're receiving.)

   c. What do you commit to doing differently as a result of having read any of the last two to three chapters?

CHAPTER 12

Bringing Issues Up So They Can Be Resolved

Your ability to powerfully, honestly, and non-antagonistically word your needs, concerns, and perspective on issues can make the difference between you getting the results you want and winding up disappointed or mired in escalating conflict.

The Bottom Line of Communication *Is* Communication

How the other person hears what you say matters as much as what you say when you seek a positive resolution.

What's the difference between the following statements?

- "You're standing on my feet" versus "You're a klutz."
- "I thought you'd be here at 2:00. What happened?" versus "You're late again. You keep letting me down."
- "You continue to ask for that; but, I've already said no" versus "You're pushy."
- "I'd like you to kiss me before you leave in the morning" versus "You don't love me."

You've answered correctly if you answered that:

- The first statements give information. The second statements attack.
- The first statements focus on performance. The second statements focus on the other person.
- The first statements give specifics. The second statements generalize.

If You Want Positive Outcomes

If you want positive outcomes, train yourself to:

- State facts, not judgments or editorial conclusions, when you express your needs, concerns, and perspectives. Train yourself to describe observable facts, as for example, "you began speaking while I was still speaking," rather than "you interrupted me."
- Focus on issues, actions, and behaviors, not the assumptions you draw about the other person. As an example you might say, "We spoke for forty minutes and you never asked how this impacted me," rather than "you don't care about my feelings."
- Be specific; the other person may interpret generalizations differently than you do.
- Don't "hit and run" by raising issues before you've taken a moment to decide how to word it for best results. Think, "What could I say that the other person might agree with?" before making any statements. For example, would the other person agree he "arrived 50 minutes late" or "doesn't respect you?" This guideline keeps you from making personal attacks and focuses you on actions and behaviors.
- If you want a result or for the future to be different, focus your energy on the improvements you want to see in the future and avoid rehashing history. In the following figure, stay to the right side of the centerline.

PROBLEM   VS.   EXPECTATION

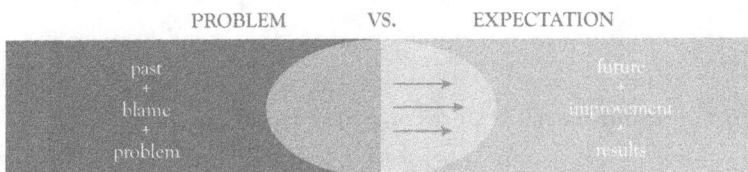

Figure 12.1 Problem versus expectation

Guardrails That Keep You Out of Trouble

The following three additional guardrails keep you on course toward a positive outcome:

- Cool down before you give feedback or raise problematic issues. At the same time, don't hold on to irritants, because they burrow under your skin and fester, tempting you to eventually overreact.
- Keep the full picture in mind—Before you tell another person what annoys you, let them know what you appreciate and value about them. Because most people hear negative remarks more loudly than positive ones, as in how loudly the "but" sounds in "you're nice, but…," you create the most effectively balanced feedback when you offer three to five positive comments to every constructively critical one.
- Stay aware: When we think only of what we want to say, we remain focused in our own brains. When you dialog with another person, observe how they take what you say. By doing so, you'll be able to calibrate if you're getting through or if their eyes have filled with tears or glazed over with anger.
- Tell the truth without judgment. If you live or work with someone important to you, be their friend in the foxhole. Be willing to speak the truth—but word it respectfully so your delivery doesn't bury your message.

Your Turn: Action Steps

Having read this chapter, take a personal inventory of your skills in bringing up issues.

1. What guidelines do you most need to remember? Is it to
   a. cool down before you give feedback?
   b. tell the other person what you appreciate and value about them?
   c. focus on the results you want, rather than history?

(Continues)

(*Continued*)

> Or, is there another guideline or insight you gained from this chapter that you want to remember?
>
> 2. Select someone with whom you need to raise a problematic issue. How will you word what you want to say factually? How will you keep yourself result-oriented?
> 3. How will you make it clear the issue you have is with the behavior and not the person themselves?
> 4. What have you learned in this chapter that enables you to proactively resolve conflict and strengthen the feeling of trust and goodwill between you and the other person?
> 5. Has reading this chapter made it easier for you to bring up problems with other people? If so, what are you waiting for before you put your insights into practice?

PART 4

Successful in Conflict

Strategies, Skills, and Tactics

In these nine chapters, you'll develop the skills and strategies to take a conflict-resolving discussion from the beginning to a successful outcome. You'll learn how to:

- Explore the stories you tell yourself that get in your way
- Own your part of the problem so it doesn't muddy the situation
- Smoothly and effectively start a conflict dialog
- Escape unscathed when dealing with toxic individuals
- Keep a conflict discussion productive even when the other person creates difficulties
- Manage fear and anger
- Apologize in a way that defuses conflict
- Get the most out of the real-life conflicts you handle
- Unravel and de-escalate conflict

CHAPTER 13

Exploring Your Stories So You Don't Trip Over Them

When we're mired in conflict, each of us tell ourselves stories about why the problem exists. These stories range from simple rationalizations to deep-set beliefs we hold about ourselves, the other person, or the way things are. Our stories provide our interpretations of the situations in which we find ourselves and the others with whom we interact. They help us explain to ourselves why events unfolded as they did and why others acted in ways that make no sense to us. While many of our stories hold a kernel of truth, the stories themselves are fiction, not fact, and can cloud our thinking.

In many of our stories, we exaggerate our own innocence, leaving out how we have contributed to the conflict, and focus on the other party's flaws. We may pretend we're helpless in ways we're not, thus powerless to solve the predicaments in which we find ourselves. At other times, we're harder on ourselves than we would be on anyone else, assigning ourselves blame we don't deserve.

Our stories form our rationale and thus trap us in rationalization. Not only do we tell ourselves stories that get us off the hook and excuse us from blame and accountability, but we replay them repeatedly in our minds until we're convinced of their truth. Our stories can blind us to information that doesn't fit our story and thus become self-fulfilling prophesies.

A Real-Life Example

Here's an example. I worked with a client who told me her manager never reached out to her to ask her view of things.

"How have you reached out to him?" I asked.

My client didn't answer but spoke again about how her manager should have sought her views. "If he had done so, these problems could have been solved."

I asked my question again but differently, "Please tell me how you reached out to him and what happened."

She looked confused, and then said, "Well, I haven't. It's not my responsibility."

How Our Stories Affect Us

As we mentally tell our stories, whether to ourselves or others, our emotions and body respond. Our temper flares. Our stomach knots. Our teeth clench. Fear jolts through us. Although we feel in control when we tell our stories, our stories ultimately control us. They dictate how we feel and lead us to act in alignment with our stories. Often, our stories fuel escalating conflict.

What Can Be Done

What stories do you tell yourself? What role do *you* play in the conflicts you want resolved?

By digging into your stories and discovering how your thoughts play a part in the conflicts in which you're mired, you gain valuable information for positively resolving current and future conflicts. For example, because you view yourself as blameless, you may shut down the potential to fix things by turning your back on the overtures the other person makes. Or, because you consider yourself powerless, you swallow words that need to be said.

Remember, your stories may be mostly fiction, developed *by you* to make sense of facts. The same facts viewed through a different lens might lead you to act in new ways. By intentionally examining your stories, you gain valuable information. No longer blinded by outdated stories, you can uproot ones that no longer serve you and would otherwise jeopardize the outcomes you achieve to real-life problems. After all, you're the air traffic controller of your mind. Thoughts don't land and take root unless you allow it.

Another Real-Life Example

Two of my clients worked well together for years. These two managers ran a small nonprofit organization and confronted many challenges together. Neither woman was perfect. Each possessed skills complementing the other's strengths and weaknesses. They became great friends.

When they reached out to me, each manager told me she had reached a point where she just wanted the other manager to leave the organization. The first manager felt the other had let her down, day after day, in the way she handled a problem employee. When I asked her why, she gave me multiple examples in which she had asked her formerly helpful colleague for assistance and the other spurned her.

The second manager felt deeply frustrated by the first manager's "blindness" to her flaws. She felt unfairly judged for trying to do the right thing for both the manager and the organization. When I asked her about it, she recounted multiple incidents in which the first manager had overreacted, creating a problem that the second manager had fixed as well as she could.

I asked each manager searching questions, enabling her to realize how each contributed to their mutual problem in a way she hadn't seen. Once each realized that there was another side to the story, they were able to repair their relationship and regain their friendship.

Questions That Help You Unravel Your Own Stories

If you want to confront your own stories, ask yourself any of the following 18 questions you believe might provide valuable insights. Please note that some of the questions require you to answer the prior question.

1. Where am I stuck?
2. What fears do I need to address?
3. What leads me to struggle?
4. What emotions drive me to act as I do?
5. What story creates those emotions?
6. What support do I need to give myself?
7. What conversations do I need to have with myself or with others?
8. How did I act in that situation, and why?

9. If I was a neutral outsider, what would I tell myself?

10. What triggers me? What is triggered in me?

11. What could I have done differently?

12. How have I justified my behavior?

13. What do I need to learn about myself?

14. What were the facts in that difficult situation?

15. What was the story I created?

16. Is there a pattern to the difficult situations in which I find myself?

17. What do I refuse to tell myself?

18. What do I need to do differently the next time I'm in a conflict situation?

The Other Person's Storyline...

You benefit as well by realizing the other person has many stories that drive their behavior. Here's a real example. As you read it, think how you might feel if you had worked with me and knew my "story."

When my first son, Joey, was born, his Apgar score of 9 (where a score of 7–10 was normal) indicated he was healthy. The hospital released us home the day of delivery because he was healthy and nursed so well.

At home, Joey seemed to smile and coo and the family and friends staying with me told me to catch a few hours of sleep, assuring me that one or another would check on him every 30 minutes.

I fell into a deep sleep and woke up with a start two hours later. I slid out of bed and leaned over the crib to look at and admire him. Something felt off. I touched Joey and found him cool to the touch. I picked him up and knew something was seriously wrong. One of my friends, a former nurse, began mouth-to-mouth resuscitation.

Joey had died despite being put to bed as an apparently healthy baby. The autopsy revealed that a certain heart valve didn't open because it was malformed. "It would have been impossible to predict," the doctors said, "without open heart surgery and there was absolutely nothing to indicate any problem."

Several years later, my daughter Jenny was born. After her birth, I didn't sleep for three days. When I realize I could no longer function without sleep, I set two alarms that went off every 15 minutes. When Jenny had even a minor cold, I had the pediatrician on call. I operated on fractured sleep.

Imagine I work with you, and you don't know my "story," but one day you say, "Lynne, I need this report." I nod that I'll get it to you, but you worry I won't get to it fast enough. You raise your voice, saying, "I need it now!" and I shriek, "Look, witch, get out of my face!"

Imagine you knew my story. Would you forgive me?

What if you didn't know my story?

Although I never shrieked at a colleague, the underlying truth of this story reminds me we need to cut each other slack. We know our own personal stories. We don't know each other's. When we experience conflict with another, we're often tangling with their past and their stories.

Your Turn: Action Steps

1. What surprised you the most as you read through this chapter?
2. Describe two stories you tell yourself. What leads you to tell each of them? What purpose does each of them serve? How might you benefit by uprooting either or both?
3. What's the most valuable insight you gained, either by reading this chapter or by examining your stories?
4. Which of the following questions do you want to keep handy, so you can regularly ask them of yourself?
   a. Where am I stuck?
   b. What fears do I need to address?
   c. What emotions drive me to act as I do? What story creates those emotions?
   d. What support do I need to give myself?
   e. What conversations do I need to have with myself or with others?
   f. What triggers me?
   g. What do I need to learn about myself?
   h. What were the facts in that difficult situation and what was the story I created?
   i. Is there a pattern to the difficult situations in which I find myself?
   j. What do I need to do differently the next time I'm in a conflict situation?

(Continues)

(*Continued*)

5. Could it be that one of the individuals you're in a conflict with has a story as impactful as mine? If you learned it, what difference would it make?

6. If you find this material concerning "stories" valuable, you can further explore it using three books listed in the resources section. *Blink: The Power of Thinking Without Thinking* reveals how each of us makes choices in the "blink of an eye." *Crucial Conversations: Tools for Talking When the Stakes are High* delves into how we see and hear and then tell ourselves a story that leads us to feel and act based on the story. *The Invisible Gorilla: How Our Intuitions Deceive Us* shows how what we expect to see becomes what we see. You might also enjoy and learn from watching the invisible gorilla selective attention test found at www.youtube.com/watch?v=vJG698U2Mvo.

CHAPTER 14

Owning Your Part So It Doesn't Muddy the Discussion

"It wasn't my fault. I blew up because I had the worst day."
"Anyone would have reacted the way I did."

When you lose your temper, shut down, or behave badly in other ways, you may feel tempted to rationalize your behavior. It can feel right to pin responsibility for your reactions on the other person or to attribute them to the situation.

When you do, you hide from the truth. *You* said what you said. *You* did what you did. You own responsibility for what you say, how you feel, and the actions you take. When you admit how you contribute to problems, you win.

Owning = winning

Consider the difference:

- "I did it" versus "you made me do it."
- "I don't like sarcasm" versus "you're too sarcastic."
- "I was angry" or "I am upset" versus "you made me angry."
- "I don't like your actions" versus "if you had any respect for me, you wouldn't have done that."

Which sounds stronger? Which feels more powerful?

When you own the part you play in initiating, maintaining, or aggravating an unresolved or escalating conflict, you increase your chances of successfully resolving any conflict. Accepting responsibility frees you to chip away at the portions of the problem you claim as yours. When you blame the other person, you give them responsibility for fixing the situation and deny your own power. You hook the other person's defenses, adding fuel to the fire.

Owning 101

If you want to take ownership, ask yourself the following questions:

- What could I be doing differently right now?
- What am I feeling, and from where did that feeling come?
- What support do I need to give myself?
- What conversations do I need to have with this other person? With myself?
- Where am I getting stuck? What am I struggling with understanding or doing?
- What fears do I need to address?
- What part of my mindset do I need to challenge?
- What do I need to learn about myself?
- What will I do differently next time?

Don't rob yourself of the opportunity to create change. Buy it, own it, deal with it, and it goes away. Deny or avoid it and it continues to lurk. Focus on your part, because that's where you have full power.

Own your piece of the action and use the power of ownership statements to resolve the conflict. Sample ownership statements include the following:

- I assure you that I will do everything in my power to get this resolved.
- I commit to working with you until we figure this out.

- I will support your efforts.
- I will take care of this by the end of the day.

Don't Over-Own: Springboard

Own what you need to change, but don't beat yourself up. You did the best you could and probably better than you credit yourself for having done. Treat each of your soon-to-be former flaws as a springboard. Forgive yourself. Let go and move on. Train yourself to say, "That was then; this is now."

Were you naïve? Admit it and educate yourself for what you need to watch out for in the future.

Do you react out of fear? Dig into the source of your fear and do what you need to move past your fears.

What do you need to learn? Realize it, embrace your new insight and immediately begin relating to yourself or others in a new way.

Say "no" to guilt and self-blame. Neither offers any positive value. Don't replay your past problem behaviors in your mind. Re-spinning situations endlessly self-defeats you by sapping the energy you need to move forward.

Partner with yourself. What do you need to admit? What needs to be said that you haven't voiced, even to yourself? What actions can you take now that will create positive change? Choose to act differently. Do you hesitate because you need to make a major change? Start with small steps.

Do you delay because you're unsure which path to take? Experiment with what works and note what doesn't work. You don't have to start out right, but you need to end up right.

A Surprising Benefit

When you genuinely own your part, the other person may do so as well, which creates a win/win situation. If not, they play a negative game you no longer play.

Your Turn: Action Steps

1. What insight did you gain from this chapter?
2. Where do you get stuck in conflict?
3. Which part of your mindset do you need to challenge?
4. What fears do you need to address?
5. Select any conflict or conflicting relationship you're currently in or that didn't successfully get resolved. What needs to be said that you haven't voiced, even to yourself?
6. What else gets in the way of your "owning" the part you play in any current or recent conflict?
7. What next steps do you plan to take?
8. Because we integrate learning best when we teach it, take any one or two useful concepts from this chapter and share them with a friend, co-worker, or family member.

CHAPTER 15

The Most Effective Way to Start a Conflict Discussion

Your first words and the tone you set when you start a conflict discussion set the stage for the outcome you'll gain. If you want a positive outcome, avoid beginning your discussion with words that create defensiveness or strike terror into the other's heart, such as "we need to talk" or worse, "I'm so angry I could scream." Opening statements like these end the conversation before it starts.

Why We Often Forget to Think About How We Open a Conflict Discussion

If a problematic initial approach torpedoes positive outcomes, why do so many of us begin the wrong way? Perhaps because...

- ☑ Emotions you've buried bubble up and burst like a flood of hot words through a dam.
- ☑ You're so focused on what you want to say that you don't pay attention to the climate you set.
- ☑ You feel so much dread about bringing up the problem that it shows on your face and seeps into your voice, which makes the other person want to back away.
- ☑ You wind up in the discussion before you're ready because something the other person says or does sets you off.

Perhaps you don't know how to start a discussion. You have several options, outlined below.

Effective Beginnings for Conflict Discussions

I start 90 percent of the problem discussions I initiate with these words: "I'd like us to have a good conversation. I'll know it's good if you feel it's good and I do as well." These words seem to disarm the other person, letting them know I care that they also feel comfortable in the discussion and hope we can partner in talking things through.

Other effective beginnings include:

- "Could we talk about what just happened?" This neutral request gets your discussion off to an immediate and factual start.
- "I'd like to hear your thoughts about…" This question invites the other person to speak before you do.
- "I noticed ____ and I was wondering what your thoughts were about it." This question invites the other person to share his or her perspective.
- "I'd like to bring something up, and learn what you think, so we can be on the same page." This opening promises a two-way conversation that ends in a mutually satisfactory conclusion.
- "Would you be interested in talking about ____?" This beginning respects the other person's choice in talking or not. If you hear "no," you can always ask, "is there a better time or topic?"

The best beginnings rest on a mutual purpose, and rather than starting with "this emotion is what I feel" or "this option is what I want," instead speak about the goals or benefits all parties to the discussion might like to achieve. As an example, you might start a contentious Board Meeting by saying, "We all care very much about our organization."

The Right Approach

When you want things to become right between the other person and yourself, begin by getting yourself right. Commit to truth as your compass and respect as your rudder. Both steer you toward success.

If you're vibrating with anger or frustration, calm your emotional storm before starting a conflict discussion. By regulating your emotions, you let the other person know that they can say what they need to without worrying you'll take their words the wrong way or use what they say against them.

Realize that the other person needs to feel there's value in the discussion and that they can also be open. By remaining honest, respectful, diplomatic, and open yourself, you fuel their willingness to engage with you similarly.

Avoid any temptation to attack the other person with blaming, judgmental statements. Remember you're not holding court—you're engaging another person in an open dialog. Even subtle judgment can hook the other person's defensiveness and launch you into battle. Respect is like air. When it's present, we don't think about it. When it's missing, we notice. When respect goes away, our discussion often no longer focuses on the original topic but becomes about respect.

Commit to be fully and individually present in any conflict discussion you open. Every conflict discussion gives you the opportunity to resolve a problem and create a new and better future.

Once you open the discussion, stick with it unless you formally say, "I need to exit this conversation." When you speak, speak for yourself. If you say you're talking on behalf of your manager or spouse, you undermine yourself, and the other person may consider you irrelevant and respond, "Let me talk with that person."

Preparation

Your preparation is crucial to your success. Outline what you want to say and the outcome you want to achieve. You might ask yourself the following questions:

- What's going on?
- Is this how I want to be treated?
- What do I want to change?
- Is this situation worth taking on?
- If so, how?

Then, set two chairs facing each other and talk yourself through an imagined interaction. Sit in one chair and begin the discussion. Then, move to the other chair and react to what the person in the first chair said. Continue this two-chair interaction by thinking what you might say and then what the other person might say in response.

To best prepare yourself, try to imagine your way into the other person's head. Look at the situation from the other person's perspective. Envision the other person adopting a variety of responses, from surprised and listening to defensive and attacking. Let yourself practice handling each potential response, including what you might do if the other person shuts down.

Spend time thinking about how the other person might interpret your statements and actions. Ask yourself, "If you were in the other person's shoes, how might you feel and react?" Remember that in conflict neither party sees everything that has happened, and so each party's conclusions are based on incomplete, often biased, reality.

During your practice, you may find yourself verbalizing inner messages to yourself. If so, transform your self-talk into positive messages such as "you got this," "right on," "you can do this," and "nicely done."

By preparing yourself, you'll develop a plan and the confidence you need to put your plan into action.

Your Turn: Action Steps

1. Have you ever started a conflict discussion with the wrong words or tone of voice and found it hard to turn things around? What made you start awkwardly?

2. How come so many people get nervous when someone else says "we need to talk," words that on their surface don't sound problematic?

3. Think of one or two conflict discussions you need to have. What words will you use to start each? Write these words out and then imagine you're the other person hearing them. How might you react if you were the other person?

4. Select a conflict discussion you need to have. Outline what you want to say and the outcome you want to achieve. Use the
   - "what's going on?"

- "is this how I want to be treated?"
- "what do I want to change?" and
- "is this situation worth taking on?"

questions to get you started.

5. Practice starting the previously developed conflict discussion using the two-chair approach. Pay special attention to your voice tone and your word choice. Continue your practice until you feel satisfied. If you decide it's too hard to practice alone, invite a friend or another person to practice with you. Once you're done, decide what you've learned from this practice that you'll be able to use when launching this discussion in real life.

6. Is there someone with whom you have a difficult relationship in part because you've overtly or subtly allowed judgmental statements into your conversations with them? If so, vow to cleanse your future discussions of those statements.

CHAPTER 16

Make It Through Unscathed When Dealing With Toxic Individuals

Len knew better than to angrily blast Jenith when she pushed his buttons. Each time, he promised himself he wouldn't do it again, but he couldn't seem to stop himself from taking the bait she tossed his way.

Vanessa promised herself she'd stand up to Ken the next time he threw his last-minute request on the top of her desk and ordered her to stop work on the other supervisors' projects. The only problem—Ken scared the heck out of her and even as she opened her mouth to insist, "I'll start on your project tomorrow," the words, "Sure, I'll get right on it," came out.

Whenever Eleanor's mom started in on her with 1990s' advice, saying, "you should do this, you shouldn't do that," Eleanor felt her jaw tighten. Invariably she'd snap back, "You shouldn't tell me what I should and shouldn't do." Eleanor hated how she reacted like a sullen teenager even when she knew her mom was just being her mom.

Have you ever found yourself in similar situations? Where, despite your best intentions, you reacted in ways you didn't intend or want? Or have you ever noticed how it saps *your* energy to be around unhappy, negative, and depressed individuals?

If so, you've experienced "matching energy," the phenomenon that explains why we "take the bait" or let another person "push our buttons."

Matching energy becomes easiest to understand when you remember how quickly you nonverbally "match" or "mirror" others, as was outlined in Chapter 10. The same mirroring phenomenon occurs with energy. Mirroring explains why an energy vampire saps your energy or why you judge or blame someone who unfairly judges or blames you. When you're around a person with good energy, mirroring also occurs but doesn't present difficulties. When you're around someone with negative energy, matching it results in your becoming part of the problem.

You can remedy this negative reaction once you realize that energy is magnetic. In the same way that magnets attract or repel, another's energy can create in you an identical or reverse match. For example, think what happened to you the last time you encountered someone who tried to control you. You might have matched the negative energy identically and dug in your heels, thereby letting the other person know there were two sheriffs in town. Alternatively, you reverse-matched and rebelled.

Here's how not to fall victim to matching negative energy:

Step 1: When you sense yourself reacting to another's energy, notice it. Then, take a slow, deep breath. Doing so helps you center yourself, so you're no longer pulled by the other's energy.

Step 2: In Chapter 6, you learned how to mentally "flash" on an image. You can use the same mental "flash" tool as an alternate focus to ground yourself in your own energy. In alternate focus, you mentally flash on an image that has a positive meaning for you. Effective images might include the face of happy baby or toddler, an exuberant puppy, someone you love, or a scene in nature that makes you feel instantly at peace.

To prove to yourself that mentally flashing on an image works, turn on the radio and notice that you can hear the dialog, and then, mentally flash on an image in your brain even as you hear what's playing on the radio. Notice as well how the image shifts your energy. A happy child's face or a beautiful natural scene may relax you. An image of a strong mountain may give you a sense of strength.

Step 3: Now that you've centered and grounded yourself, you can better tackle the problem. Even better, you may notice your changed energy influences the person you're interacting with, in the same way that their energy initially impacted you.

Once you master this, you've gained a powerful tool to emerge unscathed when encountering toxic individuals.

Here's a real-life example of how works. Let's assume, like the previously mentioned Vanessa, that your job requires you to assist three supervisors. You're working on multiple tight-deadline projects given to you by two of your three supervisors when in rushes Ken, who hands you a new assignment, and barks "Complete this immediately!"

In the past, you may have quaked inside when facing his angry intensity. Your jaw may have tightened, and your face flushed or whitened.

Imagine handling this differently. You take a deep breath and realize that Ken just barked at you. If he were a dog, would you freeze inside or think, "that's a barking dog." If the latter, you might straighten your shoulders, stand tall, and let the dog know "that's enough." To Ken, you say, "I'll get it done as soon as these two prior assignments are finished. Hopefully I'll start on it this afternoon."

If Ken escalates, demanding, "I need it done now!" you might say, "If you let Steve and Mark know your assignment needs to move ahead of theirs, and they agree, I'll put theirs' aside and work on yours."

Realizing When You've Let Another's Toxic Energy Seep Into Your Brain

Although you're learning that how you react to another person is up to you, you may occasionally let a toxic person poison you before you realize it's happening. Here are six clues you've done this:

- You regularly talk about the toxic person, their behaviors, and your feelings about them to others;
- You find your joy or sense of self-worth diminishing;
- You begin to wonder if you have the power to take them on;
- You lower yourself to their level and find yourself reacting in a way that's "not you";
- You comfort yourself with poor choices in the foods you eat or the amount of alcohol you drink;
- You let this other person impact other relationships—you find yourself erecting a wall between you and others, or you start yelling at your kids or snapping at your friends.

If this happens to you, you may need to detox yourself by taking a long walk, writing about the situation in your journal, or asking a friend to engage in a role play practice interaction with you so you can build the skills you need to differently handle the toxic person. Above all, remember you're the landlord of your mind and don't need to rent space to another person's judgments.

Your Turn: Action Steps

1. What are two situations in which you can use alternate energy? What will be the benefits?
2. Practice your breathing and mental flash the next time you encounter a situation that would formerly have upset or made you react. Notice the difference.
3. Develop two images you can use in stressful situations to provide yourself an alternate focus. Develop both a peaceful, relaxing image and a strengthening, empowering image.
4. Because we solidify our knowledge of new skills and strategies when teaching them to others, find a friend who could benefit from what you've just learned and explain it to them in your own words.

CHAPTER 17

Keeping the Conflict Discussion Productive

You launched the conflict discussion. While the discussion started out rocky, you hit your stride and felt you and the other person were getting somewhere. Then, the conversation hit a rough patch and seemed to veer out of control. When your conflict discussion slams into trouble, here's what you need to do.

Keep Your Eyes on Your Goal

You started the conflict discussion because you wanted a certain outcome for the situation and your relationship with the other person. Keep those goals in mind because they serve as the lighthouse that guides your conversational ship to shore.

Keep Yourself in Check

It's easy to let someone else's reaction, defensiveness, agitation, or belligerence knock you off balance. Your own adrenaline can hit you like a wave and can make you reactive. When an adrenaline wave hits you, don't let it throw you, but use it. Feel its impact as it hits you like a breaker and realize you are the surfboard and the wave is not you, it's what slammed into you. Notice and reverse what's happened to you. If your fists are clenched, open your hands and stretch your fingers. If your breathing becomes short and fast, slow and deepen it.

Your job? Align your behavior with the goals you set. If you want a positive, honest, open relationship, keep your words, demeanor, and energy positive, authentic, and open. If you want the other person to feel respected and be open, listen to what they say even if you don't like what you're hearing, and treat the other person's views with respect.

By maintaining awareness of your behavior, you control the one part of the conversation over which you have control—yourself.

Use Conversation Guardrails

To help maintain control over yourself, pause, take a deep breath and exhale slowly whenever you sense yourself beginning to react. Pausing activates your parasympathetic nervous system, allowing you to enjoy a quiet "rest" time. Your autonomic nervous system comprises both your parasympathetic and your sympathetic nervous system; the latter drives your "fight or flight" response during stressful situations.

During your pause, your blood pressure lowers, and you'll sense your heartbeat slowing and feel your body returning to its relaxed state. As you pause, ground yourself by feeling your feet on the floor or the chair holding you. Drop your shoulders, relax your face, and move your body into a more open state. These intentional physical gestures help calm you down and allow you to navigate through discussion danger zones.

If the person vents or hurls words at you, imagine these words going over your shoulder and not hitting you in the chest. When you don't fuel the other person's anger with your reaction, the other person generally runs out of steam.

You may find it helpful to take notes when the other person speaks. Your notetaking can help prevent you from reacting to statements the other person makes and interrupting them.

Creating a slight distance by note-taking doesn't mean you'll be numbing yourself. Instead, these strategies help you remain fully aware and present. Additionally, during the discussion, ask yourself the following:

- "What's going on in me right now?"
- "What outcome do I want?"
- "What do I want to do or say now?"

Then, bring your goal to mind: an effective two-way dialog in which you and the other person reach an agreement or a positive resolution.

Word Your Thoughts So They Can Be Heard

When you're in conflict, the other person views the current situation and past events differently than you do. Because of this, you need to explain your perspective so the other person can understand it even if they have a different view of the past and what needs to happen in the future.

You do this best when you give facts, rather than your conclusions or emotional responses. Here are two examples:

- "You spoke before I finished speaking" rather than "you're domineering," or "you interrupted me"
- "We agreed to meet at 2:00" and not "I can't rely on you."

Even in these examples, you can see how careful the word choice needs to be. "You spoke before I finished speaking" works better than "you interrupted me" as the latter might strike a defensive nerve if the person with whom you're speaking habitually interrupts.

Despite the careful wording of "we agreed to meet at 2:00," the other person may react defensively with "you always make a big deal out of small issues." If that happens, remember to keep yourself in check and use the handling yourself under fire strategies offered in Chapter 5.

You'll also want to remember the strategies presented in Chapter 12 on how to bring issues up so that they can be resolved. These strategies include focusing on behavior that the other person can change and providing expectations for what you hope to see in the future rather than rehashing history.

Make It Safe for the Other Person to Share Their Views

You can't fully fix a two-person conflict when you're the only one talking. The other person needs to feel there's a value in the discussion and that they can openly express their views. You accomplish this by committing to listen and by respecting what they say.

Even, and especially, when you don't agree with how they interpret the past or current situation, you can reach a mutual agreement more easily once you learn the other's views. You need to know:

- How they read the situation.
- What's driving them to act, say, and feel as they are doing.
- What they hope for as an outcome.

Adopt this focus on the other person's viewpoint from the beginning of your discussion. Realize that we tend to discuss problems with those who already agree with us, thus creating an echo chamber in which we hear only views sympathetic to our own. We can navigate beyond our tunnel hearing by asking ourselves, "If I was the other person, how would I want someone to approach me?" Empathy is a crucial skill; it allows us to understand how the other person sees the problem.

Pull the Other Person In

Aim for a dialog, not a monolog. Show genuine interest—after all, you want a positive relationship or at least a solid and lasting outcome. You can pull the other person into the discussion with your listening (Chapter 9), questioning (Chapter 11), and raising issues so they can be discussed (Chapter 12) skills.

Reinforce your listening with empathy statements that acknowledge you've heard what the other said and "get it." For example, you might say, "I can understand why you felt that way" or "I'm sorry you felt that way."

Sample questions might include:

- "What do you want me to do to solve my part of the problem?"
- "What did you mean by ___?"
- "What will it take for you to let go of the feelings you're holding?"
- "What will it take for you to feel this situation has been resolved?"

If the other person makes a negative statement, you can move the discussion into a positive direction by reframing it. For example, if the other person accuses, "you were incompetent," you can ask "What would you have wanted me to do differently?" or "What would have met your expectations?"

As part of pulling the other person in, don't be afraid to take responsibility for your part in creating the situation or to admit mistakes you've made. A genuine apology can open shut doors.

Practice

To prepare yourself for taking a conflict discussion through stuck points and past detours, practice. As outlined in Chapter 15, use the two-chair approach. Start the conflict discussion and switch to the other chair. Then, respond as the other person. Run through this practice three or four times, and each time have the other person react differently—defensively, aggressively, or by shutting down entirely.

After each practice, particularly the most difficult ones, reward yourself with self-talk as follows:

- "I'm getting better."
- "I did that pretty well."
- "I definitely learned from that situation. Here's what I'll do better in the next run through."

Take This Closing Step

As your final step, come to an agreement on the specific actions that need to be done to change things for the better.

Your Turn: Action Steps

1. Think back on some of your recent conflict discussions. What behaviors from the other person (i.e., aggressiveness, defensiveness, or blaming) threw you off balance?

   What have you learned or gained from reading this chapter that will help you "stay in check"?

(Continues)

(*Continued*)

2. Breathing has come up regularly as a tool you can use. Even those of us who realize the value of breathing may forget to breathe when it's most needed. How do you plan to practice breathing so it becomes second nature?

3. Select three improvement-oriented issues you want to raise with another person. Word them factually and as future expectations, rather than as problems. What impact do you think the different wording will make on the other person?

4. Practice a full conflict discussion, from start to finish, using the two-chair approach.

   After you're finished, assess how you did. What did you do well? What could you have done better? What did you learn or relearn from doing the practice?

CHAPTER 18

If You Sense Fear or Anger Rising

The twin emotions of fear and anger may bubble to the surface in conflict situations. Alternatively, fear and anger may lurk under the surface and act like riptides, pulling you under. When you can manage your own and others' fear and anger, you can resolve many formerly irresolvable situations.

The Challenge of Fear

Perhaps fear has stopped you from launching a conflict discussion or resulted in you swallowing words you needed to voice. Possibly, fear has been a slithering snake whispering "danger" in your ear. Unaddressed fear can swamp your fighting spirit and derail your ability to act in your own best interest. Worse, fear can magnetize another's aggression.

Surface Fear

When you avoid what you fear, the fear doesn't dissipate. It darkens from a shadow to a blockade.

Your path forward—pull your fears to the surface and face them.

Ask yourself the following questions:

- What fears do I need to address?
- What triggers my fears?
- What support do I need to give myself to deal with fear?
- How will it benefit me to face my fears?

Use Fear Productively

Once you claim your fear, you can use it by harnessing its power and applying its energy in a positive way. A deer that steps onto the road is alert but freezes when it faces a car's headlights. You need to be aware as well as alert—able to process clues and not just observe them. The deer needs to understand and move out of the way. Fear can heighten your awareness and sharpen your ability to see and hear. Like a caffeine boost, fear-generated adrenaline can motivate you to act.

Transform Fear

Franklin D. Roosevelt once said, "Courage is not the absence of fear, but rather the assessment that something else is more important than fear."

Once you make that assessment, can you act? Yes, and in the process, you discover courage inside yourself and triumph over fear.

Here's your "how-to" manual if you currently feel mired in fear that swamps your ability to speak and act.

Admit or own your fears. Doing so can be as simple as saying, "Yes, I feel fear" or "I'm afraid of…" or "I'm afraid that…"

Next, deny its power or hold over you. When you focus on what you fear, you lose sight of your skills and abilities. You betray yourself by backing down and away from the challenges you need to face.

Instead, tell yourself, "I won't let my fears hold me back. I'll dig into them. I'll face my fears." When you do this, you may find your fears were based on fiction and anticipated danger, and not fact.

What if you uncover perceived weaknesses or other negative beliefs about yourself along with your fears? Beliefs are not fact. Often, they're inspired by others' messages about us. At other times, they're generalizations we created to explain why bad situations unfolded as they did. Once you become conscious of your negative beliefs about yourself or the situations in which you find yourself, and their sources, you can toss many if not all of them out.

By deciding to manage your fear, you empower yourself. Fear and distrust feed on each other, and by naming your fears, you ease their grip.

When and How Do You Start?

Now.

You can't conquer fear by waiting for all your anxieties to disappear before taking a step forward. You're the pilot of your mind. You don't need to let your fear take over the controls and determine your destination. You're the air-traffic controller of your mind. You don't need to let fears land and take up permanent residence. You can tell yourself, "It's time to fly."

Are you willing to exit your comfort zone and to drop your fear baggage? In *Beating the Workplace Bully: A Tactical Guide to Taking Charge*, I challenged readers to consider how a brave person would handle the threatening situation and become that brave person. Visualize yourself as a person who has the courage to voice your thoughts and to act in your own best interest.

Allow yourself to imagine the worst that might happen. As you do so, place the palm of your hand on your stomach and breathe slowly and deeply. You may feel a knot forming in your stomach, tightness in your chest, or tears welling up in your eyes. Tell yourself it's all right to feel this way and let the tears flow. Emotions need to be expressed.

If negative self-talk whispers into your mind with statements such as "I can't do this," respond, "Oh, but I can!" Let your mind get used to the fact that you've decided you can manage whatever happens.

What if you can't? That's when you call someone you trust, tell them you need support, and talk about your fears. Their nonjudgmental listening and questioning may help you get past the barriers you've erected.

You may find that journaling helps. You can write about why certain situations hit you so hard; why you feel vulnerable; what the situation or feeling tells you; what knocked you off your feet or made you feel uncomfortable. When you ask yourself questions, reflect on your answers, and reframe situations, it helps you sort out your thoughts and emotions and allows you to make meaning from what you've experienced. As you write, or, alternatively, talk with a friend, you'll find yourself arriving at insights about what you can take from each situation.

Anger

Anger can surface in conflict situations. Lift the lid off an unresolved conflict, and you may discover you're angry at the other person or even at yourself for accepting mistreatment or allowing a problem situation to continue unresolved.

Managing and Using Your Anger

Allow yourself to feel your anger. As with fear, anger needs to be processed and integrated so it can be managed and healed. If you smother anger under a "there's no problem" facade, it turns inward and festers.

Use your anger. It can inspire you to act.

To translate your anger into effective action, ask yourself:

- At what and whom do I feel anger?
- What level of anger do I have at myself? For what?
- What underlying issues need to be addressed to enable the anger to dissipate?
- What outcome would satisfy me or allow me to feel that the situation has been resolved?
- What positive actions do I need to take?

What If Your Anger Feels "Over the Top?"

Just as a pressure cooker has a safety valve, you may need someone to whom you can express the depth of your anger, so it doesn't explode out of you, causing you to react impulsively or say words you later regret.

Facing Another's Anger

At other times, you may confront another person's anger. If you sense yourself reacting to another person's anger, take a slow, deep breath. By breathing and using the grounding techniques you learned in Chapters 6 and 16, you can avoid being pulled into heightened reaction. Even more important, you can do what most defuses another person's anger—you can listen rather than speak. Further, when you don't react, the other person often realizes they're playing handball with no wall and their venting runs out of steam.

Your Turn: Action Steps

1. Name three of your fears. Who or what are you afraid of, or what negative outcomes do you fear?
2. In what ways have your fears impacted your ability to handle conflict?
3. How will it benefit you to face your fears?
4. What beliefs do you have about your ability to handle conflict? Where did those beliefs come from? Do they serve you well, or do you need to uproot and replace them?
5. What steps do you plan to take to address the fears that block you from handling the conflicts you face?
6. What insights about your fears and beliefs surfaced as you read this chapter?
7. What did you learn in this chapter you can use to manage your own or another person's anger?

CHAPTER 19

The Right Way to Apologize

Has someone ever apologized to you by saying, "I'm sorry you took it that way"?

A real apology?

Not even close. That hollow apology doesn't express remorse or show the person wronged that the apologizer "got it." Instead, "you took it that way" blames the hurt person for how they reacted.

Fake apologizers don't admit to wrongdoing or offer to change their behavior. Instead, they justify their words or actions by clever defenses, such as "I'm sorry I kicked you out of the apartment, but I did it for good reasons," or "If you gave me greater freedom, I wouldn't have needed to be dishonest." Half-hearted apologies fall short, leaving the wronged person to work things out for him or herself.

The Power of the Apology

If you've wronged someone else, lost your cool, let another person down, gossiped about a colleague, or otherwise "blown it," your genuine apology can restore trust, end a conflict, and move a relationship forward. The honesty of an authentic apology cuts through the walls conflict and problem behavior creates.

Guidelines for Making an Effective Apology

Do you have someone to whom you need to apologize? Here's a 10-point guideline for creating a sincere, restorative apology that rebuilds trust:

1. Say you're sorry. When you say, "I know what I did was wrong," you acknowledge that your words or actions hurt the other person. Give someone you've hurt the twin gifts of empathy and remorse by saying you regret what you did.

2. Whatever you say, mean it. Heartfelt honesty rings true.

3. Admit responsibility. Don't make an excuse, justify your behavior, or otherwise shift the blame. As Benjamin Franklin said, "Never ruin an apology with an excuse."

4. Don't share blame, as in "We both said stupid things"; "I was busy and in a hurry. You know how it is; you've been there yourself," or "It wouldn't have happened except that with this project we've both committed to, I've been running on empty."

5. When apologizing, avoid "if" words such as "If I hurt you, I'm sorry." These words say you don't realize you hurt the other person but subtly blame the other person for feeling hurt.

6. Don't expect an instant reward. Don't expect the other person to apologize to you just because you've apologized to them. Give your apology as a gift you offer freely without expecting a gift in return. It can take time for walls to come down and trust to rebuild. The good news?—Relationships tested by conflict may rebuild more solidly than before.

7. Don't expect the other person to remain silent while you monolog your apology. The other person may not be ready to accept your apology and may instead confront you with anger or resentment deeper than expected. If this happens, listen. You may not like what you hear and the other's words may even be unfair, but it's better you hear the other's words and learn the status of your relationship.

8. Ask for forgiveness, acknowledging that forgiveness is a big ask. You might say, "I know it might take a while, but hope you'll forgive me."

9. Realize an apology isn't a "get out of jail free" card, nor a remedy that erases what you've done. Do your best to right the situation or at least make amends.

10. Promise it won't happen again. Say you'll change and explain how you plan to change.

A Meaningful Practice Opportunity

Would you like a chance to practice?

We all have something for which we need to apologize to ourselves. Perhaps you hold yourself to an unfairly high standard, never cutting yourself slack. Maybe you've let yourself down by not standing up for yourself. Dig deep. What do you need to tell yourself you're sorry for? How will you promise to change?

Take some time and create an apology you give yourself. Say your apology to yourself, and perhaps record it on your smartphone so you can replay it when you need to hear those words again. You can even follow your apology with a forgiveness promissory note to yourself, as writing your commitment to make changes reinforces them.

Avoid Undermining Yourself

While it's important to apologize, don't turn yourself into an over-apologizer or cheapen the word "sorry." If that's already your habit, realize you undermine yourself by excessively, unnecessarily saying "sorry." Do you recognize these common examples?

- "I'm sorry to bother you, but…" For what are you sorry— You have the right to ask questions or ask for attention. Your questions and interactions aren't a "bother."
- "Sorry, could you just look at this?" Exactly what are you sorry for? Isn't it a good practice to ask for a second pair of eyes?

If you recognize you're an over-apologizer or otherwise cheapen "sorry" by using it when you don't mean it, train yourself to replace "sorry" with "excuse me" or "pardon me." "Thank you" also works as in "thank you for your reminder" or "for your patience," rather than "I'm sorry for the delay."

Your Turn: Action Steps

If you haven't already, practice your apology skills by making one or more apologies to yourself. Review your apology against the 10 guidelines. Complete your apology(ies) with a promissory note.

1. Select one or more individuals to whom you need to make an apology and create an apology for each person or situation. This practice works even if this person is no longer in your life. Although it's better if you deliver these apologies in real life, you derive a benefit from simply writing them.

2. Now that you've created several apologies, and perhaps delivered one or more apologies, which of the 10 guidelines do you find most helpful? Are there any to which you find it challenging to adhere? What are you learning or gaining from your practice?

3. What most gripped you in this chapter? Was it longing for someone in your life to apologize to you, or the sense that you need to apologize to someone else, but aren't sure how that person might take your apology?

4. If you're a person who habitually uses the word "sorry," with what word or phrase do you plan to replace it? How will that change your communications?

CHAPTER 20

Conducting an After-Conflict Assessment

One of the fastest and best ways to develop your skills and confidence is to coach yourself using real-life lessons. In this way, you can make conflict work *for* you.

Unfortunately, many of us use what we did or didn't do in real life to beat ourselves up. We think, "I should (or shouldn't) have done that. Why didn't (or did) I?" We regret every misstep and even blow them up out of proportion. If this is your habit, be careful. Self-criticism saps your energy. While it's a benefit to admit mistakes, don't make that the end game or beat yourself up over what you did, when it was often the best you could do at the time.

We also often overlook what we did well. When we accomplish something that was a new achievement, such as breathing or restraining ourselves from not taking the bait, we devalue that achievement, thinking "that's only step one."

If the above fits you, it's time you turned this around and used every real-life lesson to power yourself forward to a higher skill level.

Your Habits

First, explore what happens to you after you experience interpersonal conflicts. Which of the following habits describe you now? Do you (select all that fit you):

a. Recover quickly?
b. Worry, agonize, or remain preoccupied with what happened?
c. Forgive yourself or the other person?
d. Bear a grudge, badmouth the other person, or blame yourself?
e. Reach out to make amends?

   f. Actively recruit others to support your "side"?

   g. Reflect on what you learned?

   h. Take responsibility and consider what you can do differently next time?

   i. Move on?

   j. Seek support from a friend or trusted colleague?

   k. _____?

Which habit(s) do you most frequently select? What's the effect of those habits? Which one(s) do you want to select more often? Now's your chance. Choose any two of the previously listed "after conflict" behaviors that you don't often utilize in real life and apply them to a recent conflict. What's the effect?

Many of the previously listed "after conflict" habits, particularly a, c, e, g, h, and i, offer value. If you chose one or more of those letters, congratulate yourself. Some offer real value but contain a downside. For example, seeking support from a friend to help you address your feelings can greatly help you, but don't let that be an end game. Because your friend has heard your perspective but not seen how you contributed to the problem, you may not receive the advice you need.

Lessons Learned

Next, create a mental or written list of "lessons learned." If you've not done this before, "lessons learned" means dissecting how you handled a situation so that you learn. Here are key lessons learned questions:

- What are/were the issues involved in the conflict?
- How did you handle yourself?
- What feelings did the conflict/situation arouse in you?
- What did you do well?
- What made the situation especially hard for you?
- What do you wish you'd done differently?
- What assumptions do you sense that you might have made?
- Were you able to show the other person that you respected and valued their thoughts, even as you disagreed with them?

- Were you able to stay in the "now" and be present during the entire discussion, or did you find yourself shutting down or disconnecting?
- What follow-up can you initiate to resolve the conflict or minimize more damage?
- What is/was your goal? What can you do to achieve your goal(s)?
- What are your insights or lessons learned? What are the deeper lessons you need to learn?

Becoming Your Own Best Coach

You'll find it valuable to let yourself become your own best coach and let real life provide the lessons you need most to learn. As your coach, remember to give yourself encouragement and support as well as improvement-oriented feedback.

When you tell yourself and others the truth without rationalizing, excuse-making, or justifying, it's freeing. Telling yourself and others the truth creates trust.

As your own best coach, ask yourself:

- What do I need to own?
- Where am I making excuses or diverting blame away from myself?
- Have I tried to make the other person wrong so I can be right?
- What does my inner voice say, and have I listened to it?
- What conversations do I need to have?
- Where am I struggling or getting stuck?
- What support do I need to give myself?
- What fears do I need to address?
- What can I learn about myself?
- What initiatives or actions do I need to take?

If you allow yourself to become your best coach, you'll grow by leaps and bounds.

Your Turn: Action Steps

1. Take a recent conflict and apply the lessons learned strategy.
2. How does it benefit you to regularly learn from real life?
3. What have you learned in this chapter that will help you recover quickly, reflect on what you learned, consider what you can do differently and better, and move on when you next experience conflict?
4. What do you still need to learn?
5. Select another conflict, choosing one you still find challenging, and try the lessons learned analysis.
6. Take the time to congratulate yourself on how far you have already come and to consider the next steps you want to take and the benefits you'll gain from moving forward.

CHAPTER 21

Unraveling Conflict

Conflict Diagnosis: Mediating and De-escalating Conflict

Conflict can be messy and difficult to resolve, especially if you don't understand where the other person is coming from. This chapter provides you with an intriguing tool, the conflict diagnosis worksheet. This easy-to-use tool helps you outline your views concerning the conflict and then forces you to look at the conflict from the other person's perspective.

Looking at the conflict from the two divergent views can provide a solid starting point for unraveling conflict. If you're someone who mediates between two individuals embroiled in conflict, you'll learn how you can use the conflict diagnosis worksheet as a mediation tool. Finally, you'll increase your understanding of actions that escalate and de-escalate conflict.

Conflict Diagnosis Worksheet

The conflict diagnosis worksheet poses six open-ended statements that help you outline your perspective on a conflict. To use it:

Select a current conflict or a former conflict that didn't resolve well and respond to each of these open-ended prompts (*Note: While you can simply think your responses, you'll gain more if you write your thoughts*).

- The problem as I see it: _____
- The conflict/disagreement I'm having with you is:

  _____

- The way I'd like the situation to be is: _____

- The way I feel about this is: _____
- What I'm willing to do is: _____
- My assumptions about you are: _____

What did you learn, relearn, or gain as you wrote your responses? If you've thought a great deal about this conflict, you might not have learned or gained any new insights. Possibly, however, you discovered you were more upset by the situation that you had thought. Perhaps you wrote that you simply wanted the other person out of your life.

Now, mentally shift and imagine you're the other person in the conflict and respond in writing to the second part of the worksheet which presents the same six open-ended prompts. As you respond, make sure you stay in the frame of reference of the other person—not as they act with or react to you, but with how they might respond if talking with a person they trust.

You may find it hard to get into the mindset of the other person. If that's true, it tells you that you'll need to learn their perspective if you want to unravel and resolve the conflict. I've found, however, that most people who take a few minutes to reflect and then begin to write know more about how the other person views the situation than they initially thought.

The Conflict From the Other Person's Perspective

- The problem as I see it: _____
- The conflict/disagreement I'm having with you is:

  _____
- The way I'd like the situation to be is: _____
- The way I feel about this is: _____
- What I'm willing to do is: _____
- My assumptions about you are: _____

As you wrote the other person's responses, what did you learn? You may have realized that the other person is equally as angry as you, or perhaps you discovered that the other person doesn't even realize there's a conflict. As I'll explain below, what you learn from writing about the situation from the other person's perspective often gives you an ideal starting point for resolving the conflict.

Two Real-Life Examples

Resolving a Marriage Conflict

I first used the conflict diagnosis worksheet when I was marriage counseling in Nome, Alaska. A husband signed up for marriage counseling. He said he loved his wife but something had happened four years earlier for which she had never forgiven him and she'd been icy to him ever since. He also said his spouse wouldn't come for the counseling because she felt that no matter how much she explained things "he didn't get it."

After he finished the first page, I asked that he put himself into the "head" of his wife and write her views. When I glanced at what he had written, I noticed he'd written, "I'm angry" in response to "the way I feel about this." I said, "That's the way she responds to you. Please get into her head. Imagine she's talking with me as the therapist. Would she write 'I'm angry' or 'I feel betrayed' or 'I feel deep sadness'?"

The husband stared at me, and then said, "I don't know what she feels." I responded, "That's a problem. However, you might know more than you think or than you're willing to admit. Try."

He sat quietly and after a few long minutes began to write. As he wrote, tears streamed down his face. When he finished, he said, "That was big." We talked briefly and then he left.

He called me the next day and said, "When I got home, I didn't open the front door. I knocked. She opened the door, looked surprised and then said, 'You finally got it.' I nodded 'yes' with tears on my face, and she reached out and hugged me. We talked all night."

The ice jam had broken.

Changing a Business Negotiation

I used this sheet myself prior to a business negotiation with a man who always slaughtered me in negotiations. I resented him because I always approached our negotiations from a "here's what I think is fair" perspective.

As I filled out the second sheet with what his response to the open-ended prompts might be, I surprised myself. I wrote, from his perspective, "She has no idea what negotiations is. She thinks she can come in with what she thinks is fair and I'll say yeah." Armed with that insight, when I met him for the next negotiation I said, "Here's my proposition" and named a figure twelve thousand dollars more than I thought was fair. To my surprise and delight, he negotiated me down to a figure twelve thousand dollars less, and exactly what I thought was fair.

I've since used the conflict diagnosis worksheet whenever I'm in a conflict in which I don't understand another person's viewpoint.

Mediation

I frequently mediate between employees sent me by their managers. I often ask each employee to fill out the two sheets. Then I ask each, "What did you learn from filling out both sheets," I often hear, "I now know more about the other person's viewpoint," or "I realize we're both equally frustrated and upset." I often begin the mediation process asking each employee what they learned. Beginning with this question and each person's answers can help the mediation start on a positive foundation.

De-Escalating Conflict

In the earlier chapters, you learned crucial skills, behaviors, and strategies that help unravel the messiest conflicts. You can de-escalate a messy conflict if you seek to understand the other person's viewpoint, using tools such as the conflict diagnosis worksheet. Additionally, you can more effectively address conflicts if you

- listen even if you don't like what you hear;
- demonstrate you're open to the other's views by asking questions and listening without defensiveness;

- re-examine your own storyline, particularly after you're given information from the other person that makes it clear you made and acted on unfair assumptions;
- are honest, kind, nonjudgmental, and empathetic;
- set up a time to discuss issues and problems;
- begin the conflict discussion by mentioning goals you and the other person have in common or by saying, "Let's look at the situation together and find a win/win solution that works for both of us."

How We Escalate Conflict—Behaviors to Avoid

Unfortunately, messy conflicts push many of us into behaviors that make the conflict worse. As you read the list that follows, you may recognize problem behaviors that you or the other person in the conflict have fallen into. Common problem behaviors include

- judgmentalness, intolerance, self-righteouness;
- letting problems fester and not discussing issues or concerns with the other person;
- building a case or gathering support from uninvolved others;
- writing memos or sending hostile e-mails;
- monologing instead of dialoging;
- seeing your problem behaviors in a favorable light, as for example, "I only got mad and yelled because the other person made me";
- deciding you need to win at all costs;
- demeaning or belittling the other person;
- showing anger, retaliating, or threatening violence.

Which of the above behaviors do you admit to occasionally practicing? The good news—when you recognize behavioral traps into which you've fallen, you can resolve to practice new skills.

Your Turn: Action Steps

1. Select an additional current or former conflict that didn't resolve well and use the conflict diagnosis worksheet. What did you learn? How will outlining both parties' thoughts make it easier for you to resolve the conflict? Given what you've learned, what are your first steps?
2. Which of the conflict de-escalating behaviors do you currently practice? Which are not part of your normal behaviors but are ones you want to adopt?
3. Which of the conflict escalating behaviors have you used? How will you keep yourself from again using them?

PART 5

Going Deeper

In these three chapters, you'll:

- Assess your conflict style
- Learn that many conflicts begin in the drama triangle
- Learn a framework for decoding personality conflicts

CHAPTER 22

Assessing Your Conflict Style

All of us have preferred habits and patterns in which we react to and handle conflict. We learned these habits and patterns early in life and they've coalesced into our chosen conflict style. Some of us quake inside and long to flee. Others seek peace at any cost. Still others instinctively respond in a toe-to-toe manner.

The following inventory gives you an opportunity to learn your preferred conflict styles and patterns. Once you identify your preferred style, in contrast with other approaches, you can add to your repertoire other styles and approaches that appeal to you.

As you take this inventory, honesty counts. Don't answer as you "should," answer as you "are." Select the alternative(s) that fits how you truly act (even if you know you should do things differently).

The Inventory

To take the inventory, read each situation, and consider the six alternatives. Then, divide 10 points among the choices according to which alternative(s) most fits you. For example, in question #1, if you really like answer "c," give "c" 10 points and the other alternatives zero. If, however, you like answer "c" but also like "a" and "b," split the 10 points, giving the most points to the alternative you like the most.

The Inventory

You glance at the phone number listed on the incoming call. You recognize the phone number of someone with whom you don't want to interact. You do the following:

Don't answer.	A _____
Take the call. You might as well handle the situation now. Besides, you think "what the heck."	B _____
Immediately think about how you can work things out and pick up the phone, hoping to ask questions, not tick off the caller, and work out a resolution.	C _____
Take the phone call because you don't want to make the caller angry, and you aren't sure there's a better option.	D _____
Take the call. After all, you handle yourself well and believe open, direct communication achieves the best results.	E _____
Take the call and if the caller gets nasty, be equally as rude back.	F _____

Total = 10

Your co-worker, employee, or supervisor yell at you in front of others in a meeting. You react as follows:

Say nothing and try to pretend it didn't happen.	A _____
Take them on directly.	B _____
Make a conciliatory statement such as "I can see your point, but..."	C _____
Nod and attempt to act with grace.	D _____
Respond "pardon me?" and then say, "let's move from this sticking place to the real issues."	E _____
Say, "Do not talk to me in a rude manner."	F _____

Total = 10

If I err, it's by doing the following:

Pretending comments and actions don't get to me.	A _____
Handling some issues before I'm ready.	B _____
Trying to make the situation work for everyone else; even if it hurts me.	C _____
Telegraphing that I'm scared or nervous.	D _____
Standing my ground.	E _____
Going toe-to-toe.	F _____

Total = 10

When criticized, I respond as follows:

Try to pretend it doesn't hurt.	A _____
Ask, "what do you mean?"	B _____
Try to work things out.	C _____
Wonder if it really was my fault.	D _____
Ask the critic to clarify their thoughts.	E _____
Let the critic know not to mess with me.	F _____

Total = 10

When others disagree with one of my ideas or suggestions, I respond as follows:

Get quiet and listen.	A _____
Point out how my ideas make sense and point out what others are not considering, but should consider.	B _____
See if I can find a way to work things out.	C _____
Worry that they'll prevail and consider how I can live with their conclusion.	D _____
Listen to their viewpoint, clarify my own viewpoint and know that we'll work it out.	E _____
Challenge what's wrong with their viewpoint and let the critic know not to mess with me.	F _____

Total = 10

(*Continues*)

(Continued)

When someone I care about or work with regularly is hostile (e.g., yells, threatens, uses abusive language), I usually handle it in the following way:

Shut down.	A _____
Let them know they shouldn't be that way.	B _____
Try to understand.	C _____
Worry what will happen.	D _____
Ask them to get to the issues.	E _____
Tell them that they need to clean it up.	F _____

Total = 10

When I walk in on a heated argument, I react as follows:

Leave.	A _____
Try to see if I can fix things and add in my thoughts.	B _____
Worry about what might happen and try to help everyone work it out.	C _____
Hope that things will blow over, particularly if those involved work close to me.	D _____
Try to meditate.	E _____
Listen, figure out what's happening, and get into the exchange.	F _____

Total = 10

When someone else takes advantage of me, I respond as follows:

Try not to deal with them.	A _____
Notice what's happening and gently but firmly let them know I don't intend to let them continue to take advantage.	B _____
Handle the situation but try to not make waves.	C _____
Worry that they'll figure out how to take advantage of me while I'm not looking.	D _____
Call the situation as I see it, calmly and without attacking anyone.	E _____
Tell them to knock it off.	F _____

Total = 10

Continued conflict seems to swirl around two employees in the department you manage (*please respond to this question even if you aren't a manager*). You respond in the following manner:

Hope it resolves itself.   A _____

Meet with each person individually and coach them so they   B _____
can learn the skills to address it themselves.

Try to make each employee feel better to alleviate morale   C _____
problems.

Ask each employee about the situation. If, however, either   D _____
tells you to keep your nose out, you back off.

Meet with each employee, assess the situation, and bring   E _____
both employees into your office for a mediation to resolve
the situation so others aren't impacted.

Bring the two employees into your office and tell them both   F _____
to knock it off.

                                                                                                          Total = 10

Conflict:

Makes you sick to your stomach.   A _____

Is inevitable and something that you need to handle.   B _____

Makes you worried and is something you would like not   C _____
to occur.

Makes you worry that worse consequences may result if   D _____
you address the conflict, even though you know you must.

Is simply part of life and although it's problematic, it can   E _____
also lead to positive change.

Is something you don't mind dealing with, although you   F _____
are sometimes too blunt.

                                                                                                          Total = 10

Total points assigned to each letter	A	B	C	D	E	F	= 100

Decoding Your Inventory

A style in which you have 30 or more points is a definite part of your pattern.

A style in which you have fewer than nine points is not part of your regular pattern.

You may have 30 or more points in as many as three patterns.

You may also have relatively equal numbers of points in four or even five patterns and have one or two patterns you never choose.

All styles have positive and negative consequences.

Some styles create significantly better outcomes, while other styles result in significantly worse outcomes.

You increase your likelihood of using the right conflict-resolution method when you feel comfortable with multiple conflict-resolution styles.

The Six Styles or Patterns

Style A: If you have 30 or more points in "A," you practice the avoidance style/pattern.

Those who avoid conflict allow conflicts to fester and escalate. Avoidance can be a legitimate choice when the issue is trivial, when you need time to think or calm down, or when heading into the conflict produces little or no payoff.

Avoiding can take the form of diplomatically sidestepping an issue, postponing dealing with a situation, or withdrawing from a problematic person or situation. As examples, in #1, you don't answer the phone; in #2, you say nothing; in #3 and #4, you pretend comments don't get to you; and in #6 and #7, you shut down or leave.

At best, avoidance works temporarily. When you regularly choose avoidance, you often let conflict continue. Worse, you may lose respect for or feel disappointed in yourself and in how others continue to behave. Because you don't stick up for yourself, you don't get what you want and need. Others may consider you a pushover and take advantage of you.

Style B: If you have 30 or more points in "B," you choose confrontation.

Those who choose confrontation have a "let's handle this" perspective. As examples, in #1, you decide you may as well handle the situation now; in #2, you directly take on the other person; and in #3, you choose to handle situations even before you're ready.

Confronters may use both negative and positive methods. Confronting can create both positive and negative consequences.

Style C: If you have 30 or more points in "C," you choose accommodation.

Accommodators live with the rules and within the parameters established by others. They hope to preserve harmony and avoid disruption. Accommodators neglect their own concerns to satisfy others' needs and believe in the "kill your enemies with kindness" approach.

Examples of accommodation include "think about how you can work things out" in #1; making conciliatory statements in #2; trying to "make it work for everyone" in #3, #5, and #7; and trying "not to make waves" in #8. Answer #9 provides a classic example of how accommodation serves as a bandage and not a permanent fix, because you try to make employees feel better yet don't address the underlying conflict.

Accommodation may prove an excellent choice when time is an issue, when the outcome matters more to the other person than you, or when the risks involved in addressing the conflict feel greater than the potential rewards. There are some discussions you're better off not having.

Accommodation may also be an appropriate choice when you wish to make a goodwill gesture or when a cooling-off period will improve your eventual results. Knowing when to let things go is as important as knowing when to engage. Sometimes you don't have the time or energy to invest in resolving a conflict.

Finally, if you accommodate too frequently, you may give up more than which you eventually feel comfortable with.

Style D: If you have 30 or more points in "D," you move forward with fear.

Those who select this pattern act, and yet worry and telegraph their hesitation to others. Because they try to appease others, others can control them.

If Style "D" is your pattern, you can grow this style into a more assertive one by honing your skills in real-life situations.

Style E: If you have 30 or more points in Style "E," you handle conflict assertively.

Those who select Style "E" approach conflict in a direct, straightforward manner. They handle issues proactively, not aggressively.

Those who select Style "E" choices consistently watch out for their own interests even as they respect others' rights. Wording that characterizes an "E" style includes "let's deal with the core issues"; "I'm standing my ground"; "I know we'll work it out"; and "I'm calmly calling the situation as I see it."

Because individuals who select the "E" style focus and address the underlying issues that create conflicts, they achieve good outcomes in most situations.

Style F: If you have 30 or more points in "F," you use a "toe-to-toe," head-on approach.

Style "F" is often selected when you, as an individual, feel fed up. If you're a manager, you select this style when you need to implement an unpopular course of action.

Those who choose Style "F" handle conflicts quickly. Addressing conflict quickly serves them well in emergency situations and yet achieves poor results in most other situations.

If you have 30 or more points in Style "F," you believe "might make right" and rarely worry about consequences. Language that characterizes this style includes "knock it off," "toe-to-toe," "do not mess with me," and "tell them that they need to clean it up." Occasionally, the unresolved issues that remain can unravel the outcome you hope to achieve.

Your Turn: Action Steps

1. Now that you've taken the inventory and learned which styles and patterns you instinctively select, along with their positive and negative consequences, you can consciously decide how you wish to change. Which styles do you want to make your own?
2. What benefits do you derive from the style or styles that form your current conflict patterns?
3. What benefits do you see to one or two other styles in which you want to develop?
4. What resources do you need to develop those patterns in yourself?

CHAPTER 23

Digging Into Where Much Conflict Begins

The Drama Triangle

We don't always know why we react to some people, nor they to us. Or why we fall into dysfunctional patterns, leading some of us to meet even minor challenges with toe-to-toe aggression and others of us to default to fear responses. Or why otherwise good people find themselves tangled in interpersonal messes.

Many of these answers lie in the drama triangle.

Understanding the Drama Triangle

Like the Bermuda Triangle, that North Atlantic Ocean region where ships mysteriously vanish, the drama triangle lurks beneath the surface of problematic person-to-person interactions. The drama triangle has its base in the matching energy phenomena you learned about in Chapter 16. It represents a three-way match of negative energy between abusers, victims, and rescuers. This three-way match includes these dynamics:

- Abusers prey on victims.
- Victims stay enmeshed with abusers (while individuals without victim energy would quickly extricate themselves).
- Victims seek out rescuers.
- Rescuers move in to help victims, and often remain rescuing, rather than finding other ways to support victims to develop their own accountability and empowerment.

The drama triangle operates like quicksand in many personal and work relationships. Even those who don't view themselves as abusers, victims, or rescuers may fall into this quicksand and find themselves entangled with others who've fallen in with them.

Drama Triangle Patterns

Abusers threaten, belittle, and intimidate those who have a default victim orientation. Few abusers see themselves as guilty, instead making statements such as "I'm angry because you make me mad."

An abuser's victim often remains enmeshed in never-ending conflict with the abuser. Those with a victim orientation take abuse to heart, accepting unfair criticism and acting as if it's true, thereby resulting in an inner powerlessness.

Victims and abusers lure rescuers into action.

Rescuers move to protect, and because they don't want others to feel bad, say and do things to make others' immediate pain go away. While this step can be a necessary, caring response when the other's pain is real, the continued "It'll be okay" or "I'll do that for you" can allow a fake victim to take advantage of the rescuer.

Rescuers who turn into enablers can leave victims in worse shape, particularly if the victim grows addicted to continued rescue.

How You May Have Fallen Into the Drama Triangle

Perhaps you came from a dysfunctional family in which a father gave you a masterclass in swaggering, yelling, and slamming his fist into the wall when he had a bad day. You may have learned to be tough yourself as a protective strategy—or discovered you could get what you wanted from others with aggression or belligerence. If so, the abuser role worked for you, and you may default to it in crunch times.

If you grew up in that same family, you may have instead responded with visceral fear and grown into an easily intimidated person unsure of yourself. When you encounter aggressive individuals, you may default to fear.

You may have wanted to protect one of your parents. If so, you may have developed into a rescuer who instinctively moves to protect others, with the need to "care take" those who need help wired into you.

Drama Triangle Dynamics

If you've encountered the drama triangle, you likely realize it's seductive and fluid in nature. For example, imagine you're a supervisor who hires an employee who lets you know they have worked for many difficult supervisors. No problem, you think. I'm a great supervisor, and this employee is a talented new hire.

You and the new employee work well together for weeks or even months. Then, one day you ask the employee to make changes or otherwise critique the employee. The employee responds, "Why are you picking on me? Are you asking everyone to make these changes?"

You're shocked. You struggle to explain why your request isn't a big deal or to tell the employee how many things the employee does very well. The employee continues to react, and you continue to reassure the employee until your improvement-oriented information falls by the wayside. The employee's reaction moved you from supervisor to rescuer.

If this situation happens several times, you may give up and not try to create more changes. You just fell into the victim role. Alternatively, you may find yourself getting angry and raising your voice. If so, your frustration resulted in your transition into abuser behavior.

In a surprising number of workplaces, a supervisor who goes overboard trying to fix things for every employee may find that an employee begins to view the supervisor as an abuser, because the supervisor "betrayed" the employee by not continuing the expected rescues.

This reaction demonstrates the fluid nature of the drama triangle, in which an employee with a victim orientation may move into abusing the supervisor by trash-talking behind the supervisor's back. Because victims assign others' responsibility, they blame and finger-point at their supervisors.

In another common example of the drama triangle's fluidity, an abuser in a domestic violence situation may cry as if they are the actual victim after beating the true victim. Occasionally, the individual who received the beating moves to comfort the abuser.

Do Any Drama Triangle Positions Prove Beneficial?

No.

Abusers need to learn that harming others destroys the healthy relationships they could have. Rescuers find a steady diet of taking care of others exhausting. Victims would benefit by stepping into their own power. Additionally, those who respond fearfully often magnetize bullies.

Exiting the Drama Triangle

How do you exit the drama triangle, given its magnetic pull? Here's how to step outside the drama triangle or escape any other negative match: find the right antidote to the negative energy.

Drama triangle energy includes the following characteristics:

- Drama—victims reacting in fear; abusers dramatically escalating; rescuers rushing in to help.
- Denial—abusers denying they treat others with contempt; victims deny they have power.

The antidote to drama and denial: reality and the truth. Here's an example. While a counselor in Nome, Alaska, I worked with a woman who'd been severely beaten by a former male friend. I helped her develop her self-confidence. One day, she told me, "I'm feeling so much stronger. I'm going to tell him to never beat me again."

I could have moved into rescue and told her that her words would likely result in a new beating. Instead, I chose to give emotional empathy without taking over and to leave the power with her. I asked questions, such as:

- "What are the benefits of your doing that?"
- "What are the potential negative consequences?"
- "What do you think might happen?"

I wanted her to reach the conclusion for herself, so that she protected herself.

When you tell the truth, speak with kindness. The truth alone can be too harsh. Kindness without truth may not accomplish the fix you desire.

Undoing the Script

What if you realize you habitually play an abuser, victim, or rescuer role? You can undo the script you play in the drama by spotting when you're slipping into a role and acting differently.

Perhaps you're a rescuer tired of caring for someone else. Instead of helping that person by taking over, could you move into the role of coach, as I did, and ask questions or offer guidance they could follow?

If you discover you're regularly caught in a "script," you may need to work on yourself. You may find it helpful to ask:

- "Where do I take over when I could leave the responsibility with others?"
- "Where do I hold myself captive in an endless rescue role?"

Because many rescuers are enablers, you may find the questions, "What truth am I hiding from?" empowering.

What if you realize you regularly respond with fear to an abuser? Start by exploring your stories, as discussed in Chapter 13, and turn your stumbling blocks into strengthening blocks. Consider what role fear has played in your life and ask:

- "What keeps me stuck now?"
- "Is it time I changed?"
- "How can I change?"
- "What are my first and next steps?"

If you use what you learned in Chapter 18, you cut the abuser's tentacles that are dragging you into the quicksand trap. When you remain grounded, and don't play the abuser's game, you deny the abuser the reward that continues the game. Instead of hoping the abuser changes, you can change and exit the triangle.

If you've spent years in responding with a default fear or victim orientation, you may benefit from strengthening your new habits by repeated mental rehearsals. During these rehearsals, imagine yourself sitting tall and making clear, direct statements. Envision yourself keeping your cool in a variety of potential trouble situations that might push your buttons. By creating the scene with as many details as possible, and putting yourself into it, you give yourself a safe environment in which to try out new behaviors. Enact the situation—visualizing yourself behaving with calm confidence so that you can feel you've been there and acted as you would want.

Has this chapter shocked you with the realization that your childhood groomed you for the role of abuser? If so, by noticing when you're slipping into abusive behaviors and deciding how to act differently, and then doing so, you can undo old patterns. By behaving differently, you build a new neurological pathway in your brain to support the new habit. Each time you repeat the new behavior, your thoughts move across this new neural pathway. As the new mental pathway becomes more frequently traveled, it becomes the route more likely to be instinctively traveled.

If you've been caught in the drama triangle, you can decide. Do you want to create new habits and behaviors? It's up to you. You can change.

The past or the future? The choice is yours.

Your Turn: Action Steps

1. Can you identify times in which you've stepped into the drama triangle? Which positions have you played?
2. What resulted when you played that position?
3. What personal or work situations does the drama triangle explain?
4. How will it benefit you to no longer remain stuck in the drama triangle?
5. What insights did you gain from the sections describing speaking "truth with kindness" as an antidote to the drama and denial?
6. If the drama triangle intrigues you, you can find interesting videos about it on youtube.com and thoughtful articles on it in the conflict section of www.workplacecoachblog.com.

CHAPTER 24

Personality Conflicts Decoded

Explaining People Who Drive You Crazy and the Ones You Drive Crazy

Do certain other people drive you up the wall? Do their actions make no sense?

Here's the reality—other people don't act the way you want or expect them to; they act in a way that makes sense to them and works for them.

As a management and human relations consultant, I conducted training sessions using all the major personality tests to help my clients understand each other. Several years ago, I spent 80 hours creating a test of my own based on the personality conflicts I'd witnessed in my (then) 35 years of consulting practice, as my doctoral work included evaluating assessment inventories. I wanted to provide my clients an easy-to-understand and remember framework detailing the four most common "types" and "operating styles" of people, along with the role these styles and types play in personality conflicts.

"Styles and Types," the inventory I developed and that you're about to take, differs from other inventories in two important areas. The four Styles and Types descriptions make immediate intuitive sense. Unlike the wonderful but complicated Myers-Briggs inventory—in which you learn you're one of 16 types—and struggle to identify which exact type another individual is—Styles and Types gives you four real-life descriptions. Also, it labels the personality type, so you don't need to remember what a "green" or a "gold" is and does.

A few things to remember:

- All operating "Styles and Types" have strengths and weaknesses.
- Our "Style and Types" framework explains how we behave and the conclusions we draw about those who walk to the beat of a different drummer.
- When we understand the style or type of others, we can relate to them better.
- The operating style and type that works for us doesn't necessarily work for everyone.

The Inventory

Assume you have 20 points to split among these four sets of words and phrases. You'll quickly discover that every set has words and phrases that appeal to you—however, you have an entire 20 points—and can give points to each of the four sets. My guess—one or two of the sets will feel more "right" to you; and one or two of the sets will click less with you. When you've made your decisions, read on to identify your "Style and Type."

Style 1:
Accountability
On time
Decision making
Commitment
Practicality
Preparedness
Responsibility
Organization
Loyalty
Realism
Consistency

Style 2

Genuine

Ideals and causes

Other people

Harmony

Nurturing

Friendship

Peace

Optimism

Trust

Empathy

Warmth

Style 3

Freedom

Risk taking and opportunities

Adaptability and flexibility

Creativity and art

Adventure

Play

Winning and competition

Spontaneity

Care-free

New ideas

Style 4

Knowledge

Vision

Problem solving

Objectivity

Competency

Standards

Insight

Strategy

Rationality and thinking

Challenge

My own standards

Deciders

If you gave the highest number of points to Style 1, you fit the "decider" category.

Deciders love structure, systems, and doing things the "right" way. They invented standard operating procedures because they want others to do things the right way—their way.

Deciders love to plan and organize, expect clearly defined expectations, and hate to leave things in flux. Once they've planned, they work their plans. If they plan a trip to Europe, they've selected the flights and hotels, purchased starter amounts of foreign currency, learned key words needed by travelers, and purchased a translator application (app). Unlike others who want the freedom to spontaneously spend an extra day in a location they especially love, deciders trade this flexibility for the security of knowing they have hotel rooms waiting for them in their next scheduled stop.

Deciders feel comfortable taking charge and generally handle leadership situations well. They make the world a better place. If they say they'll handle something, they follow through. Deciders know how to develop systems. They're the people in the school district who make sure that school buses arrive at the right time into the right places to pick up the students who need a bus ride home. Deciders love to-do lists so much that when they do things not on the list, they *add* them to the list.

Deciders appreciate traditions. If you ask them what they plan to do next Thanksgiving, they're able to tell you, because it's exactly what they did last Thanksgiving, and why do something different when what worked before worked out well?

Deciders are organized and orderly. If you peek into their closets, you'll find their clothes organized according to color, seasons, or type. They're dependable, reliable, stable, and consistent.

One Achilles' heel for deciders is how upset they get with rule violators. For example, when a decider heads into the grocery store to pick up five items, they go right to the correct shelves and waste little time. They know what they want to buy and hustle quickly to the 15-item-or-less-cash-only express line.

If they find themselves behind a shopper with a cart loaded with 26 items, they're horrified. They look up at the express sign and count the errant shopper's items again. They ask the checker, "isn't this the express line?" not because they don't know but because they want the rule violator to realize they've been caught. If the 26-item-shopper then pulls out a checkbook and starts to write a check, the decider's jaw sets. If they had needed to write a check, it would have been in their hand and prefilled, with everything but the dollar amount and signature.

Deciders can be difficult opponents in conflict situations because they feel they're right and find it difficult to change their mind once their opinion has firmed. If you want a decider to consider a new option or strategy, carefully listen to what the decider has already understood to be true, and then, look for ways in which your strategy aligns with or adds to what the decider has already determined is the right decision. Deciders respond well to those who ask them thoughtful questions and who don't expect them to completely divorce themselves from their earlier opinions.

Relators

Relators care about feelings, relationships, and how decisions impact others. They give support and understanding and depend on support and understanding from others. When others don't provide approval, support, and understanding, they keenly feel the lack. Because relators expend energy to create harmony and care about others' views, others can manipulate relators by withholding approval from them—sending relators into a "trying harder" tailspin.

Relators want you to say "good morning" in response to their morning greetings. They want others to feel supported. They wonder if there's something amiss with their co-workers or others when they don't get the same cooperative treatment they give. When I intervene in workplace situations, I often make statements to relators such as, "That person didn't mean to snub you when they walked past your 'hi' in the hallway without returning a greeting; their focus was on month-end financials."

Relators see the good in everyone and give others chance after chance. They're soft touches who cut others slack *and* worry they've done something wrong when things don't work out. Relators nurture their friends and family and can be idealistic and optimistic.

Relators hate conflict and often do everything they can to find a compromise or create harmony even as their stomachs and hearts twist in knots. Those who take strong stands find it difficult to deal with relators, saying they take flight in a fight and hide their true feelings.

Free Spirits

Free spirits need freedom. If situations or others don't offer them flexibility and choices, they create both. Free spirits push against boundaries. They don't like to be boxed in. When others say, "You need to do it this way," they think, "Oh really?" If you say, "Don't cross this line," they jump on it, asking, "This one?" with their toes resting halfway over the line.

Free spirits are rule breakers. Rules to them aren't rules, they're guidelines for others. When the decider says, "This is the way it is" or the relator says, "Everyone will feel better if you do this," the free spirit thinks, "But, do I want to?"

Free spirits take risks and love adventure and spontaneity. If you offer them a trip to Portugal costing only $500 for airfare and hotels if they head to the airport now, they immediately call an Uber, in contrast to the decider who might try to negotiate for 2 weeks to plan the trip.

Free spirits love excitement. If you drive with them on the freeway and point out there's an exit coming up, they respond, "Got you covered." While the decider has already moved over into the exit lane and the relator has moved over and is now waving other cars in front of their car, the free spirit zooms into the exit lane at the last minute.

Free spirits compete about things others don't even know are contests because they like to win. If they can't win, they often don't play. They love variety and multitask well, particularly if you give them the opportunity to choose when and how they complete each project. They're flexible, adaptable, and impulsive. Others view them as bold individuals who engage in risky decision making. While free spirits rarely make it to meetings on time, they always have a good story for what made them late.

Free spirits frequently wind up in conflict situations because they color outside the lines other draw and don't respect others' systems or rules. Relators and deciders often view free spirits as non-team players, and this view can transform conflict discussions from disagreements over decisions and issues into personal attacks and personality conflicts.

Detectives

A detective's favorite words are "why" and "Google" because they're always investigating. Natural skeptics, detectives seek proof and rationale; they value competency, reason, and logic. Because their intellectual curiosity rarely extends to people issues, detectives cause a multitude of personality conflicts that take them by surprise.

Detectives like puzzles and figuring things out, so much so that in people situations they dive over empathy into problem solving, not realizing their focus on details and questioning can make their co-workers feel blamed. Imagine a relator standing in front of a copier saying, "Darn, this copier stopped working." Eager to help, the detective launches into a series of questions beginning with "What were you doing when it stopped?"

Although a logical question and one easily answered by stating, "Trying to make a copy," the co-worker may feel blamed for having "done something" to cause the problem. Detectives need to learn that their well-intentioned interrogation can push others' buttons.

Detectives can be visionary and ingenious. They routinely improve everything they're handed. They love challenges and seek to go beyond simple answers. Because detectives have a penchant for collecting data, they can be slow decision makers, creating impatience in others who consider them overly analytical.

As you might expect, detectives wind up in a variety of conflict situations and can feel blindsided by others' frustration with them. At the same time, if others want to unravel a sticky conflict situation and need an ingenious answer, a detective may be exactly the person needed.

Your Turn: Action Steps

1. Which one or two of the four "Styles and Types" fit you best? How does this orientation impact your ability to handle conflict?
2. Bring a recent conflict to mind and decide—which "Style and Type" fits the person(s) with whom you were in conflict? How does understanding their style help you to better navigate the conflict?

(Continues)

(*Continued*)

3. Who do you know (including yourself) who fits the decider style? What have you learned that might better enable you to work with the decider in your life?

4. Who do you know (including yourself) who fits the relator style? What have you learned that might better enable you to work with the relator in your life?

5. Who do you know (including yourself) who fits the free-spirit style? What have you learned that might better enable you to work with the free spirit in your life?

6. Who do you know (including yourself) who fits the detective style? What have you learned that might better enable you to work with the detective in your life?

PART 6

Handling Specific Conflicts

Fixes That Work

The 13 chapters in this section focus on challenges that require you to use an advanced level of conflict-resolution skills. You'll find strategies you can use and ones you don't expect. Test yourself—as you read the beginning of each chapter, consider how you might address the challenge presented and see how close you come to the workable solutions offered.

CHAPTER 25

Seven Strategies for Nuking Energy Vampires and Judgmental Critics

Do you regularly cross paths with an energy vampire who sucks the good mood out of your workday—someone who lets you know they judge you and finds you lacking?

We all know judgmental critics who twist the knife into our self-esteem or cast storm clouds over our day. You can avoid the vampire and judgmental critic, shake off the sludge tossed on you, or you can … act. If you'd like to avoid the toxic riptide that energy vampires and judgers create, try the following seven strategies.

Accept What's True and Leave the Rest

Have you made mistakes obvious only in hindsight?

Of course you have. How can you stretch your boundaries without making occasional gaffes?

Unfortunately, when you work or live with judgers, they focus on every misstep you make until you feel bad, despite the progress and successes you achieve.

Strategy one—take away their power. In the same way you destroy a blackmailer's leverage by admitting the truth, admit you're not perfect. Self-acceptance powers growth. When you learn from your mistakes, you move beyond the person others judge and become a new, improved model.

Don't Collude

You free yourself from the spiderweb hypercritical people spin when you don't take negative comments personally. Those judging you and others often aim for the low blow, hitting you where it most hurts. Stop giving so much weight to others' disapproval.

When you take others' negativity to heart and won't let it go, you collude with your critics and turn a negative riptide into a tidal wave.

Keep Your Distance

Have you ever been zapped by a judgmental person and thought: "I saw that coming but didn't think it would happen to me?" Or "She gossips about everyone else, but I never believed she'd do it to me?"

If you want your good mood and job satisfaction to last, keep your distance from those who enjoy putting others down—it's just a matter of time before they slam you.

Don't Feed Critics

If you don't want to magnetize judgmental people to yourself—don't reward them.

When you observe someone making themselves feel better by making others feel worse, don't feed their venting behavior by listening. If you work with someone who assassinates others' reputations, don't give them information they can use against you.

Stay Joyful

Hypercritical people can't "rain on your parade" when the parade thrills you. What's the number 1 antidote to toxic judgmentalness?—Joy.

Focus on what's going right. What do you appreciate about those with whom you work? How have you grown? What are you doing well?

Don't let others or their criticisms drag you into their black hole where you lose focus on what's good and right.

Question Your Critics

Judgers excel at pushing you into tight corners by implying you've messed up so grievously you can't recover. Turn their criticisms back to them by asking, "What would you have me do?" Chances are they won't have an answer, because they know how to attack but not how to support.

Put Them on Notice

If you learn a character assassin has spread rumors about you, call them out. You might say, "I've heard you've said, '_____'; and if I continue to hear falsehoods like that, you and I will meet with our manager."

If a peer says to you, "Do you know what 'X' is saying about you?" respond, "Let's you and I go find X and have a three-way conversation."

The bottom line: If you work or live with individuals who scrutinize you and your actions, and regularly act like you've made a big mess, consider their judgmentalness a gift that you return to sender.

Your Turn: Action Steps

1. Select an energy vampire or judgmental critic with whom you currently or formerly interacted. What reaction do you have as soon as you think of this individual? If you find yourself pausing your breath, take a moment to breathe. You've got this!
   Now, review the seven strategies and imagine applying them to your interactions with your vampire/critic. Which ones work best for you? Which ones have you already used in real life? Which ones do you intend to use with your next vampire/critic?
2. How have you colluded with the judgmental critics in your life? What exit strategy can you use?
3. If you admit your mistakes, and accept that you weren't perfect but are getting better, how does that benefit you?

(Continues)

(*Continued*)

> 4. When you add to your sense of what's right, you create a shield against which an energy vampire's arrows bounce off. Reflect on what gives you joy or happiness. Then, the next time you know you're about to head into an interaction with a vampire or judger, bring your sense of joy or happiness with you and use it to ground yourself. Remember, you can choose—who and what do you want in your mind. You're the landlord of your mind; evict problem renters.

CHAPTER 26

Snappy Comebacks When You Need Them

The snappy comeback you wish you'd had when "Jim" sniped at you at the dinner table or in the meeting, and you sat frozen and speechless. The silencing comment you wish you'd given "Brenda" when you walked past her and another individual and overheard her dissing you.

Why don't those comebacks arrive when you need them?

Here's Why...

When you experience a verbal attack or another threat, it trips your habitual neural pathways, sending you into high-alert mode. You physically tense; you breathe rapidly and shallowly; your heart rate speeds up. You feel flushed or sweaty, may feel nauseated or a knot in your stomach, and your face may flush or whiten.

The Solution

The solution? Inhale deeply and exhale fully, thus slowing your breathing and activating your parasympathetic system. The result—your heartbeat slows down and your body returns to its formerly relaxed state.

In addition to inhaling deeply and exhaling fully, physically ground yourself. Let yourself feel your feet on the floor or notice how you feel as you're sitting on the chair. Drop your shoulders and relax your face. By relaxing physically, you look more relaxed and feel more at ease.

Your Comeback Arsenal

Prepare yourself to handle verbal attacks with an arsenal of easily remembered statements you can use.

"Give it a rest" lets a sniper and those hearing the snipe know you're calling "game over."

You can ask, "Pardon me?" as if you can't believe the gossiper or sniper meant the insulting remarks.

A calm "your point?" says you don't think the individual who attacked you or your ideas has made one.

"I'll take that under consideration" reminds the other person that you control you.

When you calmly say any of the above without any edge in your voice, it derails the sniper's charge.

The "Take Control" Strategy

When someone slams you with a putdown, train yourself to take a breath and ask a question. By asking a question, you take control of the encounter. For example, if a sniper in a meeting insults your work by saying, "This proposal isn't well thought-out," and you ask, "What parts of it do you believe need fleshing out?" you force the sniper to answer you. If you overhear gossip, you take control by saying, "Please continue. I hadn't heard that gossip about me" or "I can always use improvement-oriented advice." Remember to breathe first so you can speak in a relaxed, not snarky voice.

Your Turn: Action Steps

1. Select a past situation in which you wished you'd had a comeback. Which of the four sample comebacks in this chapter might have helped? With those four examples as a springboard, create another comeback you think might work to stop your verbal attacker.
2. If you haven't yet developed the habit of breathing when you're verbally attacked, practice deep, slow breathing in every situation in the next three days in which breathing might benefit you.

3. Imagine a situation in which someone verbally attacks you and record the attack into your smartphone. Hit "play" and practice asking the attacker a question.

4. Real-life practice: when someone snipes at you in real life, remember to breathe and respond with a comeback or ask a question. Practice this simple, effective strategy until it comes easily to you.

5. If you enjoyed this chapter, and want more, you might want to read *Beating the Workplace Bully: A Tactical Guide to Taking Charge*, as it has 235 pages of detailed strategies for outsmarting bullies and attackers.

CHAPTER 27

When a Sniper Won't Let Up

Your co-worker or family member snipes at you all day long, making you feel you're experiencing waterboarding. How do you handle it?

A Real Story

Here's what Pia wrote about a workplace sniper:

"After I returned to my office from a staff meeting where each of us reported on recent and upcoming projects, my coworker said, 'You made a mess of that.'"

"I didn't ask him what he meant, as that would have been an open invitation to him to dish out more disparaging remarks. He snickered, and while I tried to ignore him and focus on my work, his snickering every thirty or forty seconds grated on me."

"I finally gave in and asked, 'Can you stop?'"

"Sorry, it's just so funny."

"I again resolved to ignore him, but he knew I could hear him. Then he said, 'The break room's latest rumor is you're sleeping with the maintenance supervisor.'"

"At that point I lost it, yelled at him to just stop it, and went home early."

Let's assume you face a situation like Pia's and have tried the normal solutions.

Initially you pretended you didn't hear your co-worker when he made nasty comments. He then escalated, repeating what he initially said louder, until you gave in and spoke to him.

You tried diplomatic truth, telling him his constant remarks bother you. In response, he said, "You took offense? You can't take a joke? My bad!"

Because the situation continued, you went to your supervisor. You didn't get the help you needed.

You spoke to HR and asked to be moved to another work area, even a closet, only to be told no viable alternate work area exists.

You've asked for remote work, but your job duties don't allow it.

You've considered quitting, except you like your job and aren't willing to leave a good job because of this sniper.

Here's what works when you want to end a sniper's games.

Stop Rewarding

Snipers watch their victims for signals that their comments have struck home. When you pretend you don't hear your sniper, he knows you have. The sniper saw your face flush, your jaw or lips tighten, or shoulders raise.

If you want to ignore a sniper, really do so. Here's how. Let your mind flash on the face of a joyous baby or a peaceful site in nature. Do you relax?

Now, let yourself hear one of the sniper's comments and notice your breathing. If you're like most people, your breathing becomes rapid and shallow, and your chest tightens.

Except, let yourself hear the comment while you breathe slowly and deeply and bring that relaxing visual to mind. Continue to flash on that visual in your mind even as you allow yourself to notice your breathing exhalation in the way you would watch a wave moving away from the shore. Continue focusing on your breathing and notice your inhalation as part of the same seashore wave-like process.

As your breathing slows, imagine your sniper's comment again, louder this time, however, concentrate on your breathing and the relaxing image. If you can do this, you'll change your reaction to one that no longer rewards a workplace sniper.

Turn the Tables

Snipers love playing "one up," but hate being bested. Take the fun out of your sniper's game. Create an arsenal of comments that let him know "game over."

When the sniper next makes a comment, couple your relaxed breathing and mental vacation with a "done and over" phrase such as "Give it a rest" or "Don't you have any new material?" Let the sniper know his gibes no longer work that he's become both boring and laughable.

Document

If you face a workplace sniper and turning the tables and eliminating his reward doesn't work, give HR or your supervisor evidence rather than anecdotes on your next visit. Your sniper's comments about your mythical sleeping around, if frequent, may constitute illegal sexual harassment. Start pressing your smartphone's record button when you return to your work area. Provide your HR office a fact-based case.

Let your supervisor hear the same recordings and let him know your sniper erodes your productivity daily. Make the problem a bottom-line productivity concern for your supervisor and no longer a "you" issue.

The result—when you effectively handle a lowlife sniper, they look for easier targets elsewhere.

Your Turn: Action Steps

1. Do you face a sniper at work or in your home? What have you tried to resolve the situation? What has resulted?
2. Practice the breathing/visualizing technique when you're not around the sniper, and then try it out the next time you're around the sniper. What is the result?
3. Memorize one or more comebacks such as "Give it a rest" and "Don't you have any new material?" Try your favorites, along with slow, deep breathing to relax you, when your sniper next attacks.
4. If you face a workplace sniper, collect documentation and visit HR or your manager.

CHAPTER 28

When You're Thrust Into an Important Role in Which Your Ability to Navigate Conflict Might Mean Life or Death

It Might Happen to You

Sometimes you take on work for which you aren't paid—because it matters, or because you've been talked into it. Perhaps you serve on the board of a nonprofit corporation, one that serves the homeless or abused women or those in need of medical or mental health services. Possibly you run for your condo association's board of directors because you want some control over the condominium unit in which you live. Despite the zero pay, you occasionally face situations that require hard work and take every ounce of conflict navigation skills you possess. For many of these organizations, decisions made by the board can result in life or death for those the organization serves.

A True Story

In June 2021, condo association board members throughout the country wondered "what have I gotten myself into and do I have the necessary skills?" The story that awakened their fears was one that shocked the nation. One-hundred and forty-five people were dead or buried under rubble when the Surfside Condo collapsed. We all felt for the victims who went to sleep in a dwelling with idyllic views, only to awaken to a nightmare.

What happened? Why did the resident-led association that operated the condominium fail to take swift action when an engineering firm told them their building had "major structural damage"? If the media accounts can be believed, the seven-member condominium board became mired in a contentious debate.

According to a well-researched investigative newspaper account, "ego battles," "undermining" of other board members, "gossip," and "mistruths" all played a part in the board's inability to decisively act.

Condo association board members, unrelated individuals who have agreed to share responsibility for their condo, face many challenges when conflict arises. The decisions board members make impact their residence, family, and finances, making the situation uniquely personal and giving individual members the feeling that the position they take should prevail. Some board members may taste power for the first time and slip into destructive behaviors.

Solution

Here's what to understand and do if you serve on a board mired in conflict.

Realize you need to exercise the highest level of skill you possess when those you interact with have fewer skills or feel unwilling to use them.

Make respect your rudder and honesty your compass.

Cut others, but not yourself, slack, understanding that emotions can impair others' cognitive faculties.

Set up a time to meet and frame the discussion your board needs to have as working together to achieve a shared goal. Before launching into the discussion, agree to meeting guidelines designed to keep emotions from hijacking the discussion.

Create a foundation of shared understanding by allowing every member to voice their thoughts and by collaboratively pouring over relevant information.

As a group, decide on your common goals and identify key issues. Discuss all key issues, starting with the least controversial first.

Listen to others' perspectives. Assume you have something to learn from those who see things differently. Try to see the situation from their perspective and to understand their rationale.

When you speak, choose neutral words. Ask questions, demonstrating your intent to understand and to dialog. If you sense yourself becoming frustrated by others' stubbornness, challenge your mindset and think past your blind spots. Focus on how to solve problems, rather than whom to blame. Remember that accusations lead to retaliation and that winning at all costs means someone loses.

It will take years to unravel all relevant pieces of the Surfside Condo story. Meanwhile, you may choose to serve on a nonprofit or condo association board because the organization's mission matters to you. You may find yourself engaged in a conflict that takes all your skills. If so, realize the problem situation gives you a chance to act in the best interests of those you serve and use all your skills.

Your Turn: Action Steps

1. Have you ever wanted to, or do you now serve, on the board of directors of a nonprofit corporation or condo association? If so, what's your takeaway from this chapter?
2. What is the impact when you respect others, even when they don't appear to "deserve" respect?
3. Why does every board member need to have and use excellent conflict navigation skills?
4. If you enjoyed this chapter and the other 12 chapters in this "Handling Specific Conflict: Fixes that Work," you might enjoy and find valuable *Solutions: 411 Workplace Answers and 911: Revelations for Workplace Challenges and Firefights*. It has a 4.7 out of 5 rating on Amazon and includes 65 of the best columns written during a 20-year span.

CHAPTER 29

Let Go of What You Can't Control

A Problem Not of Your Making

Have circumstances ever mired you in a problem not of your own making? Here's what Jenn wrote:

"I knew I might regret telling my manager the truth. I just didn't know how much. The problem is and has always been my co-worker 'Steven.' He's a cheat. He doesn't work the hours he claims on his timesheet."

"Steven set up an e-Bay resale brokerage when the pandemic started. It was easy for him to hide his moonlighting when we worked remote. Now we are all in a work-hybrid workplace. On our three days back in the office, it's more obvious he's not working. Also, multiple co-workers give Steven things to sell."

"This week, our manager twice noticed Steven wasn't at his desk. When my supervisor asked me where Steven was, I said, 'I don't know.' I didn't. I didn't tell him what I speculated. But he wouldn't let it go. He insisted I answer and asked, 'Where do you think Steven is?'"

"I don't know."

"Where do you suspect?"

"It all poured out. I didn't want to 'out' my co-worker, but his lack of integrity made me sick. I also realized if I didn't say something, I was letting Steven get away with cheating."

"Then, my manager asked me to keep an eye on the situation. He said Steven cheated in a way that was hard for him to prove, and he needed concrete evidence because Steven was a member of a different race and might claim racism. He said for him to make a solid case against Steven, someone had to notice when he wasn't at his workstation, and then look around and spot that he was hiding out on other floors in the building, doing personal business."

"I told him I wasn't a spy." He said, "Just tell me when Steven vanishes, and I'll send someone else to locate him."

"I don't know how Steven found out I'd told on him, but he did. He's now at his desk full-time."

"The problem? Steven's personable and has many friends in the office. They benefit from his e-Bay business. They're mad because Steven shut down selling co-workers' things just before Christmas, when they could really use the cash."

"Steven also convinced our co-workers he never spent more than a few minutes during the day on e-Bay because he automated things, and just splintered his thirty-minute lunch break throughout the day."

"They don't sit next to him and realize he's been on his personal cell and computer almost all day. They feel I've wronged Steven and have iced me out. How do I combat this?"

Solution

Realize Others Don't See What You See

I told Jenn she could ride out this office storm.

I asked her to realize her co-workers didn't understand the big picture and likely believed what Steven said. I added that Steven tapped into their self-interest, and they likely admired his entrepreneurial success.

Avoid Landmines

I told Jenn to avoid three landmines.

First, no matter how tempted you feel to explain what's really happening, keep your ego in check and bite your tongue. Steven has protected himself by creating a positive office persona. Even if you have the facts and others don't, those who like Steven give credence to what he says and consider you mean-spirited. I explained that while she might feel every one of her co-workers thinks she's the problem; mature employees realize there's more to a story than one person's side.

Second, don't isolate. When you do, you eliminate the opportunity for your co-workers to see you as the person you are. Engage with your co-workers, even those who view you with suspicion. If you continue playing your "A" game, some of your co-workers may wonder if they've been played—by Steven.

Third, don't regret when you take an action you believe is right. Stand up for yourself by not letting toxic behavior of any kind get to you. A proverb says, "Above all, guard your heart, for everything you do flows from it." When you're judged negatively by others, it's easy to let that poison seep into your mind. Let go of what you can't control and remember you did the right thing.

Your Turn: Action Steps

1. Have you been in a situation you couldn't control?—In which others saw a different picture than you? What was it? What landmines have you stepped on?
2. In what ways does realizing what you're up against help?
3. How come it's important not to isolate?
4. How is it a benefit when you stand up for yourself by not letting toxic behavior get to you?
5. Why does letting go of what you can't control help you?

CHAPTER 30

When You're Up Against a Street Fighter

Do you face a street fighter? Street fighters, those who survive by fighting dirty, bait you, hoping you'll trip into a trap so they can take you out.

Here are the traps you need to avoid:

Trap 1: Denial

When a street fighter attacks you, a million thoughts run through your mind, such as "This is unfair, and everyone will realize that." "All I need to do is wait this out." The opposite proves true. Your inaction lets the street fighter know that you'll go down easy. If a street fighter launches an attack on you, you need to deal with it, or you allow him free rein.

Trap 2: Reaction

Like mosquitoes that fuel themselves on human blood, street fighters feed off your reaction to their words and antics. Don't reward a street fighter by reacting—or you give him energy. If he baits you, you can always respond, "Nice try, didn't work."

Trap 3: Collusion

If you swallow an attacker's judgments or allow a street fighter to shape how you see yourself, you aid and abet him and become less of who you are. You wouldn't let another person stomp on your foot or physically slam you off balance. Don't let a street fighter bump into and push you over inside your head.

Trap 4: Delusion

Hoping for good treatment from a street fighter because you act professionally is like entering a ring with a bull, believing he'll treat you well because you're a vegetarian.

Trap 5: Stooping

Street fighters have years of experience, giving them the advantage if you climb into the ring with them. Don't let a street fighter push you into unprofessional acts that you'll later regret.

Trap 6: Appeasing

Street fighters love to make others back down. Don't be afraid to firmly and professionally dish out negative consequences to someone who attacks you. Give a street fighter or any other bully an inch and he becomes your ruler.

Trap 7: Chasing

Street fighters excel at launching salvos over the bow, leading you to spend energy chasing trumped-up issues while the fighter perfects his onslaught. Don't reach for everything tossed at you by a street fighter. By disengaging, you give the street fighter less attention and therefore less power.

Your Turn: Action Steps

1. Have you faced a street fighter? If so, into which traps did you fall?
2. How come it's so important to not ignore or deny what's happening when you're attacked?
3. What have you learned that helps you not react when you are attacked? Sometime this week, when you face a small or large attack, use those strategies to maintain your equilibrium.
4. What have you learned that helps you avoid colluding with a verbal attacker?
5. How come appeasement doesn't work?

CHAPTER 31

When You're Chairing a Meeting and a Hothead Challenges You

Here's the question a department manager posed:

"One of my employees, Eric, loves challenging ideas voiced by other employees or myself in meetings. This morning, he slammed the proposal put forward by another employee. That employee is also a hothead and argued back."

"I told both employees to stop. Neither did. Eric, however, raised his voice and then challenged me. I raised my voice to take control of the meeting."

"It was a mess, and I didn't like the person I became when I angrily reacted to Eric. What should I have done instead?"

Solution

If you're chairing a meeting and an employee challenges an idea voiced by you or another employee, defuse potential conflict by asking the employee questions to ensure you and others understand the employee's views. Once the employee has explained, summarize what the employee has said.

Then, allow others to put forth their views.

If you're chairing a meeting and an employee challenges you, say, "Let's take that offline after the meeting."

If the employee persists, tell everyone else, "Offline just started. Could the rest of you leave us?" By letting everyone else leave, you spare them the time waste and conflict.

Later, you can resume the staff meeting, with or without this employee.

Your Turn: Action Steps

1. What makes it essential to maintain your cool when you're chairing a meeting?
2. What is the reason we don't like the person we become when we raise our voice in reaction to a hothead raising their voice?
3. What makes it a good idea to say, "Let's take that offline after the meeting?"
4. What makes it a benefit to ask even a hothead questions to get their views on the table?
5. Which of the strategies presented in this chapter do you like best, and where can you use them?

CHAPTER 32

Resolving Conflicts in a Virtual Work Environment

"We had a situation blow up this morning," the CEO said when he called. "It came out of nowhere. One small issue, a manager not letting his peer know about a meeting, unleashed a tidal wave of anger from her. We talked to the first manager. He said he'd accidentally overlooked putting the other manager on the Zoom invitation. He reminded us that the second manager hates meetings and complains about how many she is forced to attend."

Conflicts flourish in a virtual work environment. Rarely do explosions come out of nowhere.

Why Conflict Explodes in a Virtual Environment

Virtual and remote work environments can become Petri dishes for conflict. When we work with co-workers and managers located at the same worksite, we have easy access to each other. We can drop into each other's offices if we have questions or want to talk through mutual projects. We casually run into each other at the coffeepot and get a sense of each other as people.

When we work remotely, we have fewer opportunities to develop rapport. When we communicate by way of e-mail and text, we can't see each other's facial expressions, nor hear the other's tone of voice. If the e-mail or text sender is someone who is stressed or gets immediately down to business without an initial, "Hi, hope all is well," their messages can come across as abrupt. If we're stressed as well, we can take offense. Testy e-mails devolve into grudges.

Unaddressed Conflict

Unaddressed conflict festers, derailing projects, eroding morale, and increasing stress for both involved parties and those watching from the sidelines. Left unchecked, conflict escalates, and can rip a team to pieces.

Fixes

Wise managers work to prevent and resolve escalating conflicts. Here's how:

If the organization can afford it, bring the company or team together in a face-to-face kickoff or annual meeting. Load these meetings with activities during which employees get to know each other.

- Model direct, positive communications.
- Resolve brewing conflict. Like rancid chicken, conflict doesn't improve when put aside for later.
- Develop managers' and employees' communications and conflict-resolution skills.
- Create team norms such as the "24-hour direct rule"—if you have an issue, raise it within 24 hours and by phone, rather than e-mail.
- Hold regular team meetings. Let your employees know you want them to voice how they see issues during these meetings, and not in the hallway afterward. If you sense unspoken issues, open the door to hidden concerns with comments such as, "What problems might this proposal create?" or "I sense some of you have concerns. Let's raise and discuss them."
- If a conflict continues, pull the involved parties into a meeting or video call. Establish meeting ground rules and let each party tell their story for others to both listen and hear. Facilitate a discussion in which the parties come to an agreement.

In the real-life situation presented in the beginning of this chapter, I challenged the CEO, saying, "You said this blow up came out of nowhere."

I then said your manager may have spoken honestly when he said he innocently forgot to put the other manager on the Zoom invite. At the same time, his response doesn't explain the other manager's tidal wave of anger. Does she have an anger management problem? Or have small unresolved incidents created a tinderbox that led to this omission igniting? This manager gives you a clue the latter might be the truth when he reminds you that the other manager complains about meetings.

Here's what I suggested to the CEO—investigate this further yourself and train your managers to resolve conflicts when they're small, before they fester and explode.

Your Turn: Action Steps

1. If you work in a virtual or hybrid workplace environment, what conflicts have you seen erupt? What led to them?
2. If you're a manager, which of the fixes have you employed? Which ones do you like that you haven't yet used? If you're not a manager, which fixes do you hope your manager will use?
3. What are your thoughts about the 24-hour rule? What problems would it fix?
4. The remote/virtual workplace section of www.workplacecoachblog .com has 35 other articles that might interest you.

CHAPTER 33

Defeating a Verbal Attacker's Three Favorite Weapons

Verbal attackers wield weapons enabling them to dominate and win. If you've been on the wrong end of their blame/shame, insult barrage, or public humiliation weapons, you know how devastating these weapons can be.

The good news?—When you understand these weapons, you can defeat them and claim victory.

Weapon #1: The Blame/Shame Game

Why does a verbal attacker explode in rage?—According to the attacker, you made them explode by screwing up or challenging them.

What happens if you ask the attacker how come they trashed you to your boss or in front of others? "It was your fault," says the attacker.

Verbal attackers excel in projecting their shortcomings on their targets. If you're the target, the attacker may even lead you to wonder what you've done. Don't go there. No one deserves being attacked. When you let a verbal attacker convince you that you're the problem, you allow the attacker to get off the hook. Instead, learn to view the attacker's blame/shame game as projectile vomit. See the problem and let it drop to rest at the feet of your attacker.

Weapon #2: The Insult Barrage Game

Attackers launch with a barrage of caustic comments that chip away at your and other targets' confidence. Even if you initially deflect the first insult, enough insults can twist you in emotional and mental knots. Soon, you're exhausted, increasingly less prepared to handle the next onslaught.

Learn to greet an attacker's comments wearing your game face. Then douse them with reality or a prepared arsenal of flattening anti-dote statements. Creating a game face becomes critical because your facial reaction, whether you turn white or blush, or look flustered, rewards the attacker. Looking as if you can't believe the attacker would have said something so stupid denies the attacker their desired outcome.

So you don't need to think on the spot, pull from your tool kit of prepared statements. Statements such as "Pardon me?," "Give it a rest," and "Is that the best you can come up with?" tell attackers their tricks have no traction with you.

Weapon #3: Trapping You Through Public Humiliation

Attackers know they can humiliate you and other targets by publically accosting you. Don't let the pressure of watching eyes freeze you into immobility or foot-sweep you into reacting.

Instead, realize you can turn the situation onto your attacker, allowing those watching to see the attacker for whom and what they are. Train yourself to ask, "Is that the best you can do?" or "Does it make you feel good to try to make me feel bad" when an attacker accosts you in public. While others look on in surprise, you'll see your attacker scramble to retake control.

Do you deal with a verbal attacker? Don't play the attacker's game or play by the attacker's rules, and you can claim victory.

Your Turn: Action Steps

1. Which of the above weapons have been used on you?
2. What benefit will you receive by not absorbing blame when it's thrown at you?
3. What benefits would you receive if someone insults you and you simply respond, "pardon me?" or "give it a rest"?
4. How might it help you to not react when a verbal attacker tries to humiliate you in public?

PART 7

Finishing Touches

Congratulations. You've learned a great deal about yourself; learned critical conflict resolution skills, and significantly improved your ability to navigate conflict. The next chapter invites you to formulate your game plan for using and continuing to develop your conflict resolution skills. In the final chapter, you'll have an opportunity to consider what you've done in the larger context of what's happening in our communities and world.

CHAPTER 34

Your Game Plan

This chapter is all about you. You've learned a lot and relearned much that you knew but weren't using when you most needed it. You've discovered a great deal about yourself that will help you navigate further challenges.

What You've Gained

You've learned that when you avoid conflict, it provides only temporary relief, and so you've worked to develop conflict-resolving muscles. You've learned to handle yourself under fire and created a "you" who stands up for yourself. You've developed skills for professionally handling criticism, attacking comments, and anger—whether it's yours or another's.

You've developed conflict-defusing skills such as listening and mirroring. You've learned how to bring up issues so they can be resolved and how to question to surface issues and create reconsideration.

You've dived deep into fear, the stories you tell yourself, and the drama triangle.

You're learned to "own" your part of the problem and the right way to apologize. You've discovered how to escape unscathed when dealing with toxic individuals. You've assessed your conflict style and learned a framework for decoding personal conflicts.

Making further changes is all about you, and the work you choose to do. What's on your list? What do you want to continue to do well? What do you want to do better, to change, or improve? What will start doing, stop doing, do less of, and do more of?

What's your commitment to yourself?

Your Turn: Action Steps

1. What has changed for you since you started reading this book?
2. Where do you want to go from here? What do you want to achieve?
3. How will you motivate and inspire yourself?
4. How will you hold yourself accountable?
5. If you haven't already, address the questions asked in this chapter's last paragraph. What do you want to continue to do well? What do you want to do better, change, or improve? What do you want to start doing or to do more of? What do you want to do less of or stop doing?
6. What's your commitment to yourself?

CHAPTER 35

Just in Time

Our world is in conflict. As I write this chapter, Russia has invaded Ukraine, and the rest of the world has watched in horror as innocent people starved and were killed. We've suffered through the pandemic, made more difficult by the conflicts between those who believe in vaccinations and masks and those who don't. Racial and political conflicts have exploded.

Who and what can turn around what's happening in our world? If your answer includes each one of us learning to handle conflicts at the one-on-one level and in our families, workplaces, and communities, you're spot on.

Conflict offers us no options. We're going to experience it. Our only choice—how will we deal with it? Will we hide our heads and let others walk on us or manipulate us into silence? Fumble through problem situations, making them messier?

When you chose to read *Navigating Conflict* you said, "no" to those options and chose instead to learn skills, strategies, and tactics to directly face and resolve conflict. You found your inner strength and courage and developed your conflict muscles. You may even choose to become someone who teaches how to conflict. Godspeed.

Your Turn: Action Steps

1. How will you make the world a better place?
2. How will you make your world a better place and the one in which you thrive?

Resources

Arbinger Institute. 2018. *Leadership and Self-deception*. Farmington, Utah, Arbinger Institute.

Arbinger Institute. 2019. *The Outward Mindset: Seeing Beyond Ourselves*. Farmington, Utah, Arbinger Institute.

Chabris, C., and D. Simons. 2010. *The Invisible Gorilla: And Other Ways Our Intuitions Deceive Us*. New York, NY: Harmony.

Cloke, K., and J. Goldsmith. 2011. *Resolving Conflicts at Work: A Complete Guide for Everyone on the Job*. San Francisco: Jossey-Bass.

Curry, L. 2006. *Solutions*. Anchorage, Alaska: Communication Works, Inc.

Curry, L. 2016. *Beating the Workplace Bully*. New York, NY: AMACOM.

Curry, L. 2021. *Managing for Accountability: A Business Leader's Toolbox*. Chicago: Business Experts Press.

Fisher, R., and D. Shapiro. 2005. *Beyond Reason: Using Emotions as You Negotiate*. New York, NY: Penguin Group.

Fisher, R., and W. Ury. 1991. *Getting to Y.E.S.: Negotiating Agreement Without Giving In*. New York, NY: Penguin Group.

Gallo, A. 2017. *HBR Guide to Dealing with Conflict*. Boston: Harvard Business Review Press.

Gladwell, M. 2007. *Blink: The Power of Thinking Without Thinking*. Back Bay Books.

Havel, P. 2019. *Arsonist in the Office*. Franklin, TN: Clovercroft Publishing.

LaBorde, G. 1987. *Influencing With Integrity: Management Skills for Communication and Negotiation*. West Wales: Crown House Publishing.

Laborde, G. 1995. *Influencing With Integrity: Management Skills for Communication and Negotiation*. New York, NY: Crown House Publishing.

Lulofs, R., and D. Cahn. 2000. *Conflict From Theory to Action*. Needham Heights, MA: Allyn & Bacon.

Medea, A. 2004. *Conflict Unraveled: Fixing Problems at Work and in Families*. Chicago: PivotPoint Press.

Patterson, K. 2013. *Crucial Accountability: Tools for Resolving Violated Expectations, Broken Commitments, and Bad Behavior*. New York, NY: McGraw-Hill Education.

Patterson, K., J. Grenny, R. McMillan, A. Switzler, and L. Roppe. 2002. *Crucial Conversations Tools for Talking When Stakes Are High*. New York, NY: McGraw-Hill Education.

Patterson, K., J. Grenny, R. McMillan, and A. Switzer. 2005. *Crucial Confrontations: Tools for Resolving Broken Promises, Violated Expectations, and Bad Behavior.* New York, NY: McGraw-Hill.

Reina, D., and M. Reina. 2006. *Trust and Betrayal in the Workplace: Building Effective Relationships in Your Organization.* San Francisco, CA: Berrett-Koehler Publishers, Inc.

Reina, D., and M. Reina. 2010. *Rebuilding Trust in the Workplace: Seven Steps to Renew Confidence, Commitment, and Energy.* San Francisco, CA: Berrett-Koehler Publishers, Inc.

Runde, C., and T Flanagain. 2010. *Developing Your Conflict Competence: A Hands-on Guide for Leaders, Managers, Facilitators, and Teams.* San Francisco, CA: Jossey-Bass, John Wiley & Sons.

Runde, C., and T. Flanagan. 2007. *Becoming a Conflict Competent Leader: How You and Your Organization Can Manage Conflict Effectively.* San Francisco, CA: Jossey-Bass, John Wiley & Sons.

Runde, C., and T. Flanagan. 2008. *Building Conflict Competent Teams.* New Jersey, NJ: Jossey-Bass.

Ursiny, T. 2003. *The Coward's Guide to Conflict: Empowering Solutions for Those Who Would Rather Run Than Fight.* Chicago: Sourcebooks.

Ury, W. 1993. *Getting Past No: Negotiating in Difficult Situations.* New York, NY: Bantam Books.

Voss, C. 2016. *Never Split the Difference: Negotiating as If Your Life Depended on It.* New York, NY: Harper Business.

About the Author

Lynne Curry, PhD, is the President of Communication Works, Inc. (Anchorage, Alaska), the Founder of www.workplacecoachblog.com, and was the Founder and CEO of The Growth Company, Inc., a nationally respected management consulting company she started in 1978 and sold in 2017.

Curry has taught field-tested conflict management skills and strategies to thousands of business owners, executives, managers, supervisors, and employees. She's well known as an "organizational fire-fighter and crisis manager" who takes on large-scale projects where the organization is in crisis and much change needs to be made quickly and well.

Curry has directly worked with more than 4,400 organizations in Washington, Oregon, California, Alaska, Hawaii, Connecticut, Arizona, Michigan, Washington D.C., Illinois, New York, Arizona, Colorado, Texas, Florida, Japan, Korea, China, Guam, and England. Her clients included the World Bank, the U.S. Department of Defense, ConocoPhillips, and British Petroleum.

Curry has qualified in court as an expert witness in the areas of management, best practices, HR, and workplace issues.

Curry's weekly blog, www.workplacecoachblog.com, has 2,497 subscribers from 130 countries.

Curry is the author of *Managing for Accountability: A Business Leader's Toolbox* (Business Expert Press, 2021) and *Beating the Workplace Bully: A Tactical Guide to Taking Charge* (AMACOM 2016). Curry has authored three earlier books: *Won By One* (Communication Works 1996), *Managing Equally and Legally* (McFarland & Company, 1990), and *Solutions* (2006 and 2014 Communication Works).

Curry is on the Editorial Advisory Board for Plain Language Media and publishes a monthly column in both Law Office Manager and Medical Office Manager. In addition, Curry has published hundreds of articles in print and online media, including inc.com, sheknows.com, workingwomen.com, and U.S. News & World Report.

Curry has written a weekly Dear Abby of the Workplace newspaper column for 41 years (adn.com) in newspapers in Alaska, Washington, and Illinois. Curry has been interviewed on radio shows and stations such as the Voice of America, KBYK, KSKA, and KNBA on topics such as "Resolving Workplace Conflicts" and "Outsmarting Workplace Bullies."

Curry has been interviewed on Monster.com podcasts as well as on television stations ABC/FOX, KTUU, and KTVA.

Lynne served as the Chair for Alaska's Labor Relations Agency under two governors.

Curry has a doctorate in social psychology from Union Graduate School-West, a Senior Professional in Human Resources Certificate from the Human Resources Certification Institute, and a Senior Certified Professional Certificate from the Society for Human Resource Management.

Curry has three children, Ben, Jenny, and Joey; three grandchildren, MaHayla, Cooper, and Parker, and two collies that she hikes with daily, Zeke and Gabriel.

Index

OTHER TITLES IN THE HUMAN RESOURCE MANAGEMENT AND ORGANIZATIONAL BEHAVIOR COLLECTION

- *Innovation Soup* by Sanjay Puligadda and Don Waisanen
- *Change Fatigue Revisited* by Richard Dool and Tahsin I. Alam
- *Versatility in the Age of Specialization* by Angela Cotellessa
- *Championing the Cause of Leadership* by Ted Meyer
- *Embracing Ambiguity* by Michael Edmondson
- *Breaking the Proactive Paradox* by Tim Baker
- *The Modern Trusted Advisor* by MacKay Nancy and Weiss Alan
- *Achieving Success as a 21st Century Manager* by Dean E. Frost
- *A.I. and Remote Working* by Miller Tony
- *Best Boss!* by Ferguson Duncan, Toni M. Pristo, and John Furcon
- *Managing for Accountability* by Curry Lynne
- *Fundamentals of Level Three Leadership* by Clawson James G.S.
- *Emotional Connection: The EmC Strategy* by Gershfeld Lola and Sedehi Ramin

Concise and Applied Business Books

The Collection listed above is one of 30 business subject collections that Business Expert Press has grown to make BEP a premiere publisher of print and digital books. Our concise and applied books are for...

- Professionals and Practitioners
- Faculty who adopt our books for courses
- Librarians who know that BEP's Digital Libraries are a unique way to offer students ebooks to download, not restricted with any digital rights management
- Executive Training Course Leaders
- Business Seminar Organizers

Business Expert Press books are for anyone who needs to dig deeper on business ideas, goals, and solutions to everyday problems. Whether one print book, one ebook, or buying a digital library of 110 ebooks, we remain the affordable and smart way to be business smart. For more information, please visit www.businessexpertpress.com, or contact sales@businessexpertpress.com.

www.ingramcontent.com/pod-product-compliance
Lightning Source LLC
Chambersburg PA
CBHW061218220326
41599CB00025B/4674